ADLARD COLES CLASSIC BOAT SERIES

Wooden Boatbuilding

build • restore • maintain

Jean-François Garry

ADLARD COLES NAUTICAL
LONDON

Published by Adlard Coles Nautical
an imprint of A & C Black Publishers Ltd
36 Soho Square, London W1D 3QY
www.adlardcoles.com

ISBN 978-1-4081-2853-4

First published in 2009 as Guide de la construction en bois © 2009 Chasse-Marée/Glénat

A CIP catalogue record for this book is available from the British Library.

This book is produced using paper that is made from wood grown in managed, sustainable forests. It is natural, renewable and recyclable. The logging and manufacturing processes conform to the environmental regulations of the country of origin.

Typeset in Rotis Sans Serif and Goudy Old Style.
Printed and bound in India by Replika Press Pvt Ltd.

Note: while all reasonable care has been taken in the publication of this book, the publisher takes no responsibility for the use of the methods or products described in the book.

CONTENTS

FOREWORD

THIS BOOK IS AIMED at all those who want to learn how traditional boats are built, either out of pure curiosity or because they have a wooden boat and wish to understand construction methods and be able to maintain their craft without making a mistake. It is also aimed at those entering into discussion with the boatbuilder who is undertaking the repair of their boat, and it will be particularly useful to those about to launch into the construction or restoration of a small wooden boat; a boat of classic construction built entirely from solid wood or using modern wooden boatbuilding methods: unsheathed strip-planking, contemporary strip-planking, clinker planking or plywood planking glued with epoxy.

The book is designed above all to be efficient and practical. It gets to the point, in a helpful manner, by deliberately overlooking difficulties that an amateur would not encounter in the restoration or construction of a small craft. The boat's construction process is explained in a logical sequence, from start to finish, from the boat's construction plans through to her launch. The many drawings and photographs enable the reader to visualise the processes better.

This brief introduction to wooden boatbuilding will, I hope, inspire the most exacting to find out more by consulting the scholarly treatises on construction and carpentry listed in the bibliography.

Traditional boats very nearly vanished. The first to be affected were all the old sailing work boats, each so different from one port to the next. Then yachts, which were built of wood until the middle of the last century, were swept aside by the flood of modern plastic yachts. Even the smallest boats, hundreds of which formed part of the landscape in ports, gradually gave way to modern glassfibre designs.

Those who truly appreciated beautiful wooden boats were no more than an insignificant minority and the last remaining boatbuilders were closing their workshops due to a lack of business. Slowly, though, people began to realise what was being lost, and the heritage, which was synonymous with traditional working boats and classic yachts, was saved, along with the knowledge, techniques and the sometimes extremely ancient customs linked to them.

The last surviving traditional wooden craft have been restored; the most exceptional of them have been assembled in museums, while others have taken to the water once again, assembling on the finest summer days here and there, to enable crews to share experiences. The public comes out in force to admire them and the fondness for them translates into a huge wave of support: today visitors to the large gatherings of traditional boats are in their millions.

There is a big difference between curiosity and passion, but amongst this immense crowd, some will take the step of increasing the circle of traditional boat fans. One day perhaps they will even join the group of those for whom the passion carries right the way through to building or restoring their own boat with their own hands.

INTRODUCTION

STEP-BY-STEP CONSTRUCTION

TRADITIONAL WOOD CONSTRUCTION

In this book we'll be tackling the principles of construction, first of all from a theoretical and general viewpoint for all boats, then from a more practical perspective, following the examples of three constructions of varying difficulty, which make up the main thread of the work: a round bilged boat (two versions), a V-bottomed hard chine boat and a flat bottomed hard chine boat.

For each construction stage, the techniques for dealing with the materials and methods are outlined in a simplified manner, but sufficient for a conscientious amateur to undertake the construction of a boat for which the level of skill needed is similar to that in the examples.

RESTORING A WOODEN BOAT

It's easy to assume that restoring a wooden boat is a much simpler and quicker undertaking than building one from scratch. This is generally true if the restoration concerns only a few defects: replacing a plank, a rib, a floor timber. On the other hand, if the restoration involves a wider range of things, for example a large section of the keel, frames or the planking, the difficulty can be just as great, if not greater than a complete new build. Indeed, you may have to dismantle the old sections, which are sometimes difficult to access, and the order in which you dismantle the boat may force you to interfere with other sections that you don't wish to replace and which it is imperative you don't break. A restoration often has more (bad) surprises in store than a new build.

You will certainly have to plan the work, taking into account the known proportion of parts to be restored and their accessibility. Each person will have a different opinion on the validity of the restoration, but even if the condition of the boat is very poor, you may overcome these challenges for the sake of heritage or the boat's emotional value.

All the construction techniques described in this guide are applicable to the restoration of a boat. Some specific methods, peculiar to restoration work, are introduced when necessary.

MODERN TECHNIQUES WITH WOOD

Alongside traditional wood construction, each stage is discussed in terms of modern woodworking techniques: eg lamination, plywood, unsheathed strip-planking, contemporary strip-planking and the use of modern glues and resins. Such techniques and materials may go against the grain for traditionalists, but can be of great value to 'broadminded' amateurs, who will find much of interest in this book.

ROPEWORK AND SAILMAKING

One chapter is devoted to rigging, ropework and sailmaking: including the latest ideas for rigging the boat before her launch and first sea trials.

MAINTENANCE

The book ends with a little advice about maintenance. In order for a boat to last a long time, the wood needs regular protection. We often overestimate the time spent on painting or varnishing work, but when such work is done on a regular basis, with the appropriate products and using the techniques peculiar to wood, the investment in time is controllable. Far from being a chore, it provides a number of sailors who love their boats with an opportunity to make their first contact with them since the winter lay-up, the moment the weather improves. This is all the more true with smaller boats, such as the examples here.

CHOOSING THE BOAT

The construction of a boat begins with questions and a decision. What boat? For what purpose? What kind of sailing? In what region? On which sea? With which crew? You need answers to all these questions if you want to find the perfect companion. In the range of boats dealt with in this book – dinghies and small sailing boats – three types or styles are covered: regional small craft, small yachts and small working boats.

TRADITIONAL SMALL CRAFT

Directly inspired by small fishing boats used along the French coasts and characterised by an extraordinary variety of shapes, they are intimately linked to a place. Someone who wishes to participate in a localised cultural movement or be integrated into the local traditional boat fraternity may well opt for one of these, and those who simply love boating, little jaunts and fishing will be in their element.

SMALL YACHTS

Generally of lighter construction, they have a style which is both classic and universal; they belong to a design group we refer to today as 'classic' yachts, that's to say refined finishes, perfect varnish and, to be successful, they also require a high level of build quality. Above all, these yachts are designed for a quiet sail or for racing.

SMALL WORKING BOATS

Often inspired by traditional workboats, but having a lighter construction, their finishes are now more yacht-like than workaday. The finest examples of them are built of solid wood, however a number of people these days call upon more modern materials like plywood, unsheathed strip-planking or contemporary strip-planking.

The four plans chosen as examples in this book are deliberately on the borderline between these various styles. They originate from local craft, well suited to sailing in the 'traditional working boat' spirit. A beautifully crafted finish will enable at least the first two to rank as classic small yachts. You may well find them all at traditional boat gatherings.

PLANS OF THE BOAT

All boats, even the simplest of shapes like flat-bottomed boats, are first drawn as a profile and a sectional view, which reveals their characteristics: varying degrees of length, beam and depth.

If shapes are more sophisticated, it becomes necessary to draw them with more accuracy on a genuine three-dimensional plan and to make a scale model.

For all boats, the build must begin with a general definition of the shapes and dimensions, which depend on the sailing use, the number of crew and, in the case of traditional boats, local cultural references. After that, the design work enables us to gradually specify the boat's shape, the details of her framing, the joints and the construction methods.

In the past, yards often preferred to build boats from a half model. For the amateur builder, whose ambition is to design a boat by referring to a traditional model, it is necessary to know how to read old plans well, to understand the way they are drawn or to draw up plans by taking the lines from a boat that already exists.

LINES PLANS

The plans of a boat are made up of her flat representation in a three dimensional format. The simultaneous reading of the three views enables us to understand the general form of the hull.

THE BODY PLAN

This depicts the sections from ahead and from astern, most often half of each view combined in the same drawing, and it generally uses the stations of the boat's frame timbers and ribs.

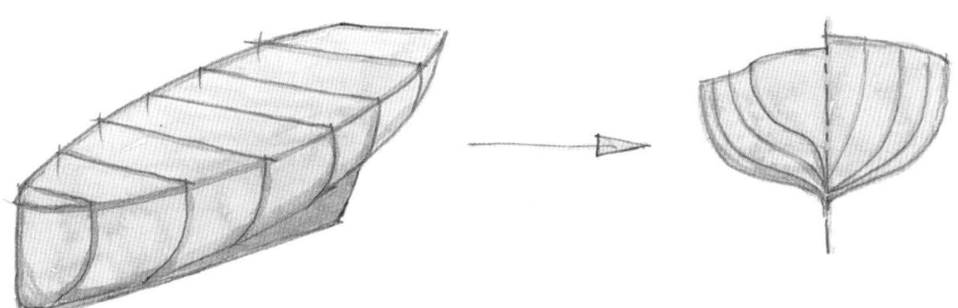

PLAN VIEW

The hull is viewed from above or from below, although these two views may be combined in a half-breadth plan. The plan view shows the longitudinal horizontal sections; if one of these is at the waterline, the plan shows her shape as she floats 'to her marks'.

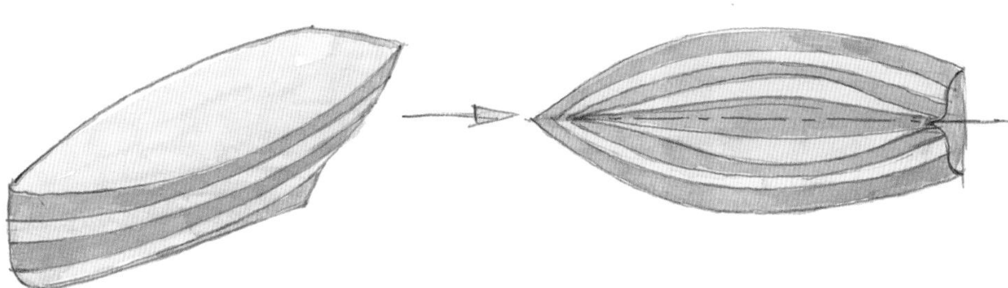

THE PROFILE (SHEER) PLAN

This drawing shows the outline of the boat. It is a side view of the longitudinal vertical sections – fore and aft parallel to the centreline.

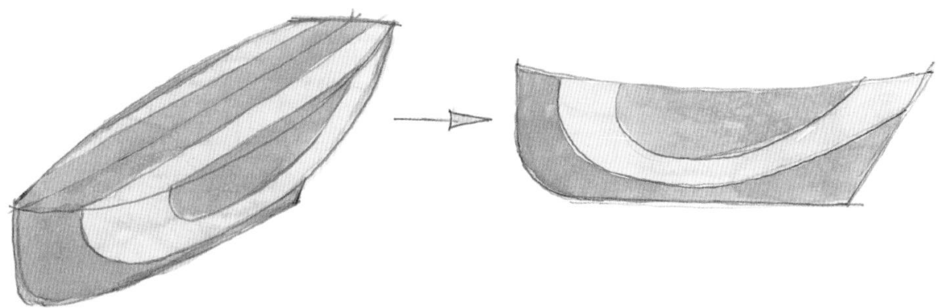

HOW TO READ A PLAN

Each of the sections represented in one view can be found in two other views.

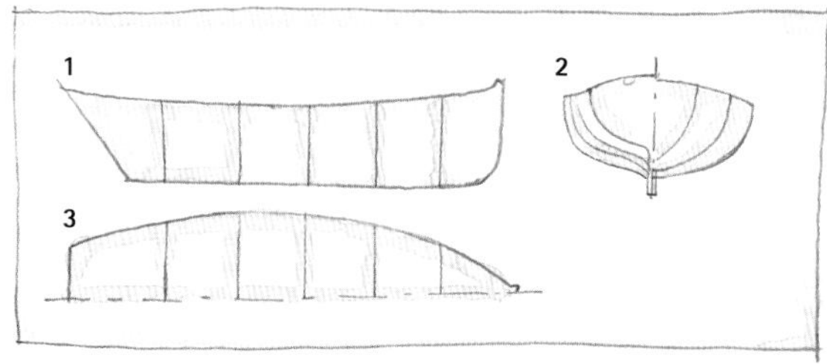

1 Section stations on the profile view
2 Section stations on the body plan
3 Sections stations on the plan view

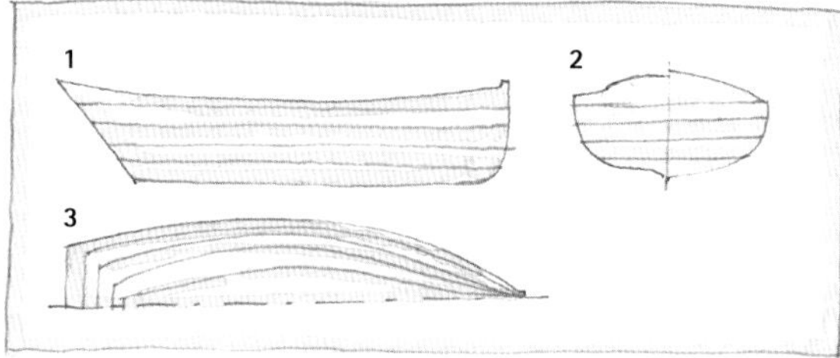

1 Waterlines on the profile view
2 Waterlines on the body plan
3 Waterlines on the plan view

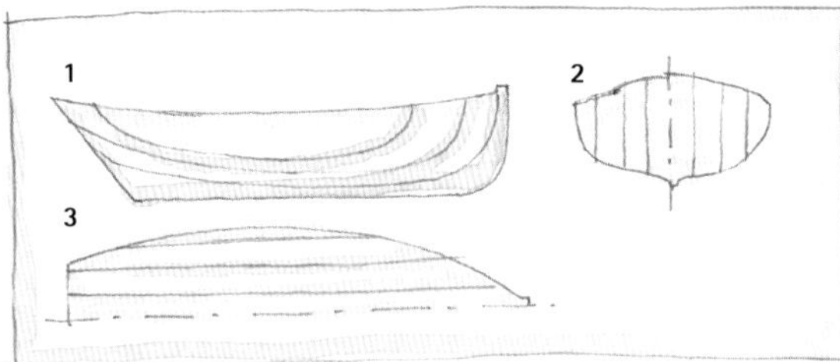

1 Buttocks on the profile view
2 Buttocks on the body plan
3 Buttocks on the plan view

In a complete set of lines drawings, these three views are superimposed to present the boat's shape in three dimensions, known as her 'form'.

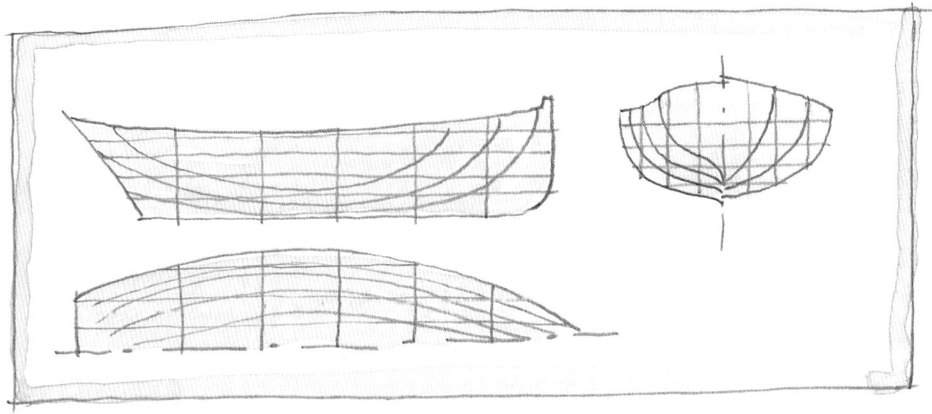

CHOOSING A DESIGN

Building a boat requires us to have the plans beforehand. These should include drawings such as those we have just described, as well as a construction plan, which indicates the scantlings (see Glossary p112) and shape and position of the component parts. Such plans may be ordered from a naval architect, who will design them according to the wishes of the person placing the order. It's the method generally chosen for a boat of some importance built as an individual craft and for all those built as a production series. The hull form calculations require skills that are generally beyond the abilities of an amateur builder.

In the case of very small craft, things are presented differently. The majority of local boats formerly built by yards haven't been designed by an architect: they are the result of a slow evolution over several generations of sailors, boatbuilders, sailmakers and riggers, who have combined their experience, observations and knowledge to eventually produce a boat meeting the local working requirements. Such a boat type was attached to a port or a whole region, whilst another (very different one) will have been introduced a few miles away to satisfy other working conditions.

All local traditional boats belong to a collective heritage in which each person is free to seek out their own inspiration. The plans proposed by way of example in this book result from this approach.

The round bilged dinghy is inspired by craft that are seen in their hundreds all the way along the French coast. The long keeled version is very suitable for setting pots or a net and trailing a line; the second version, with a centreboard, serves as a tender or a recreational boat in her own right. This type of hull has evolved as much for sailing as for rowing.

The V-bottomed hard chine boat is a simplified version of the round bilged dinghy. It retains the form and general shape, but is adapted to a less complicated hard chine construction. Though aesthetically 'crude', the way such boats function with oars and under sail remains identical.

The flat bottomed hard chine boat is an even simpler craft to construct. The shape enables the craft to be used for rowing and, possibly, sailing if a centreboard is added.

These plans, which are only examples, may support all kinds of adaptations or transformations.

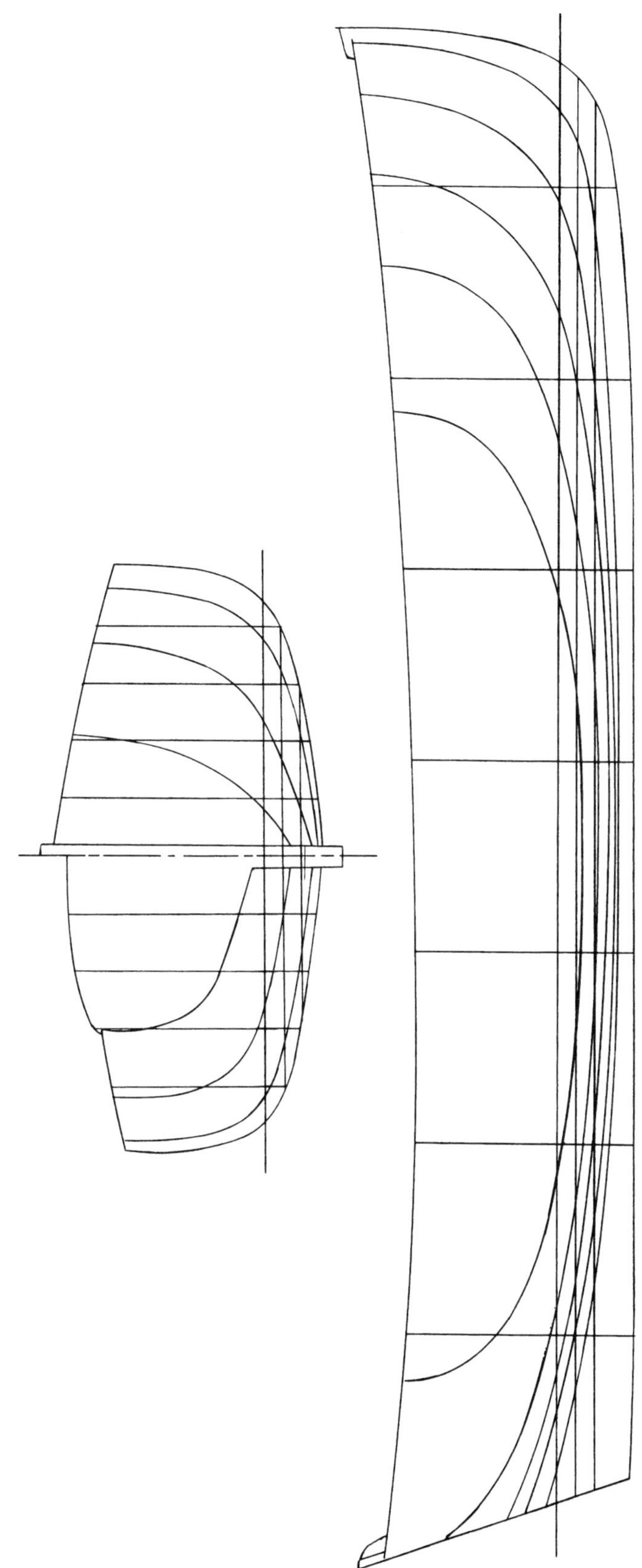

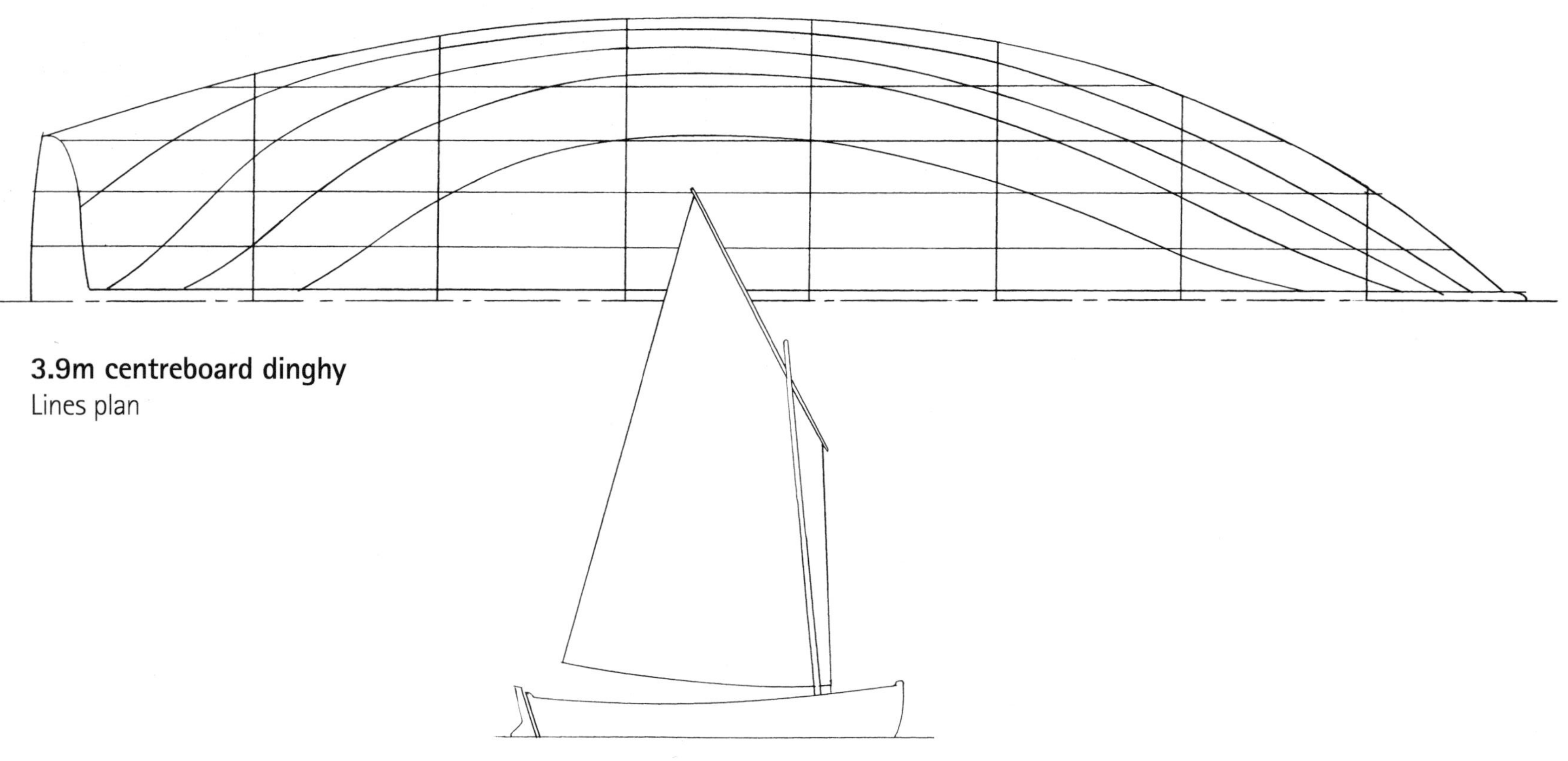

3.9m centreboard dinghy
Lines plan

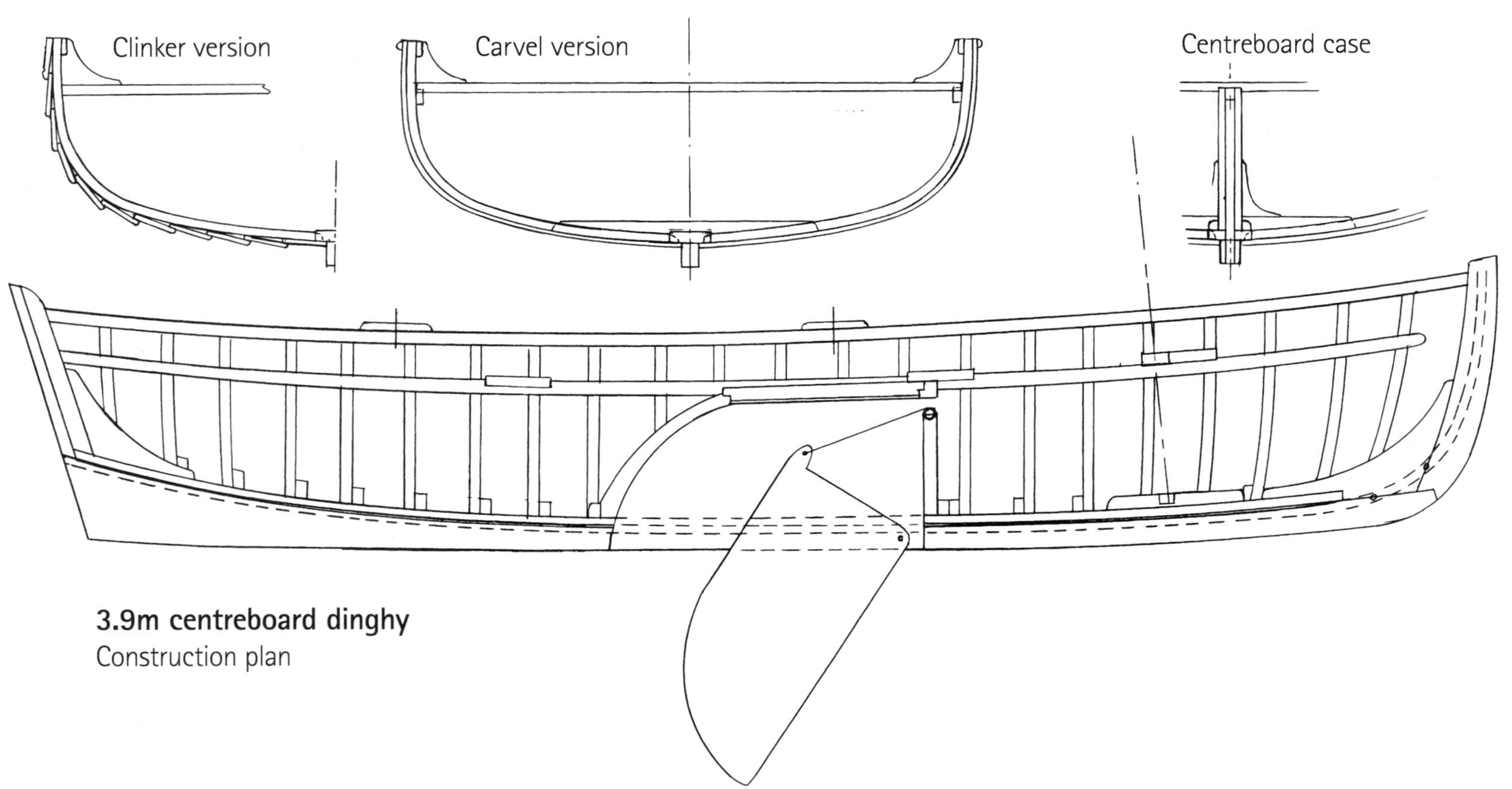

3.9m centreboard dinghy
Construction plan

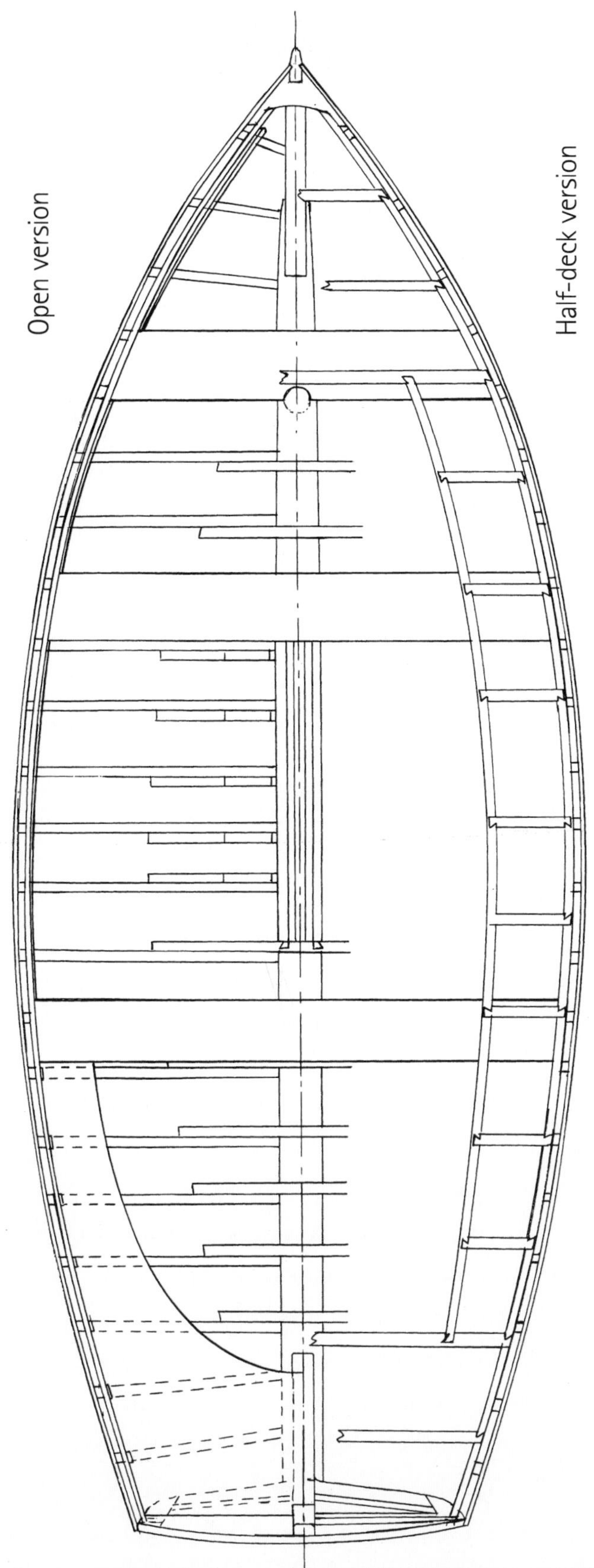
Open version
Half-deck version

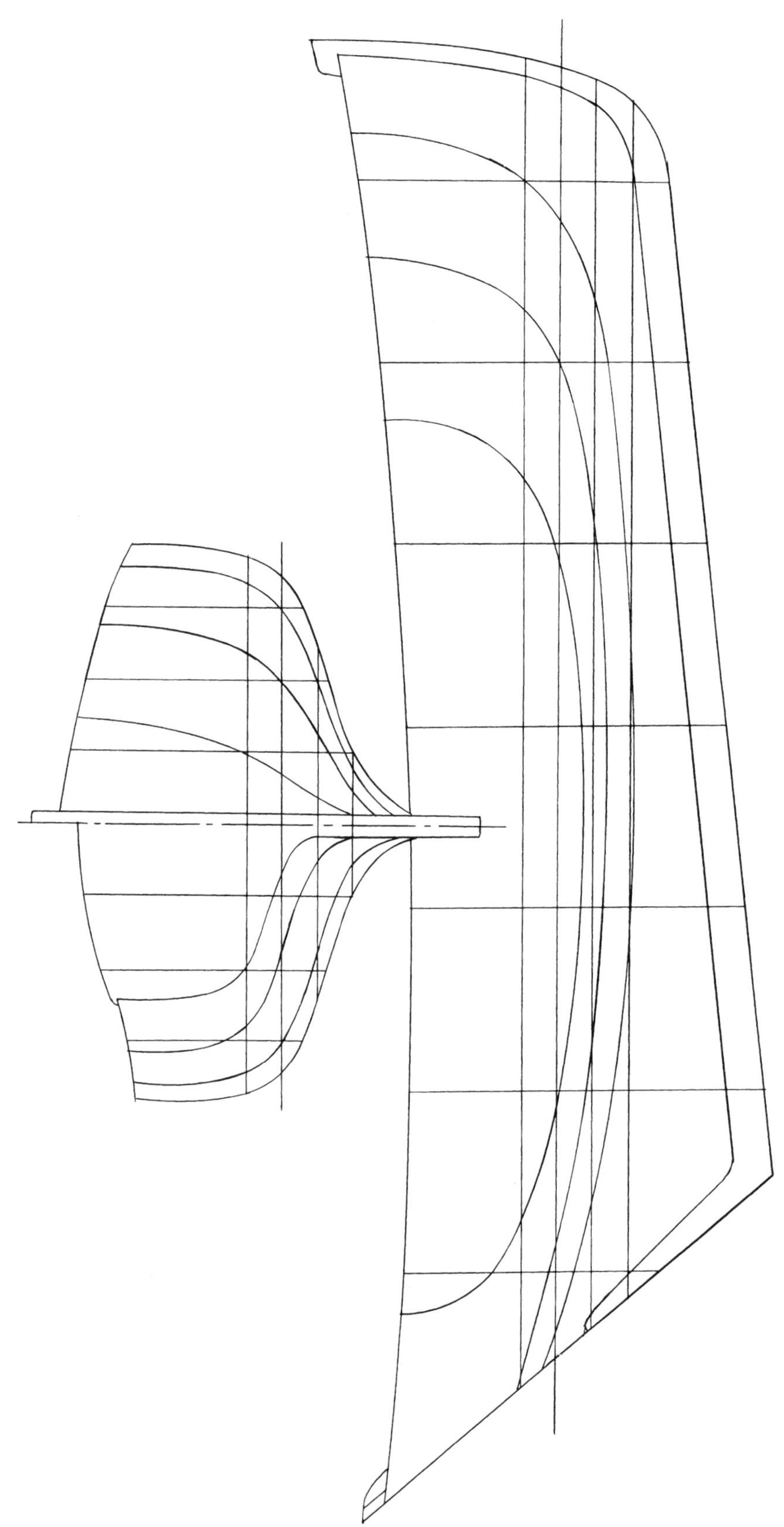

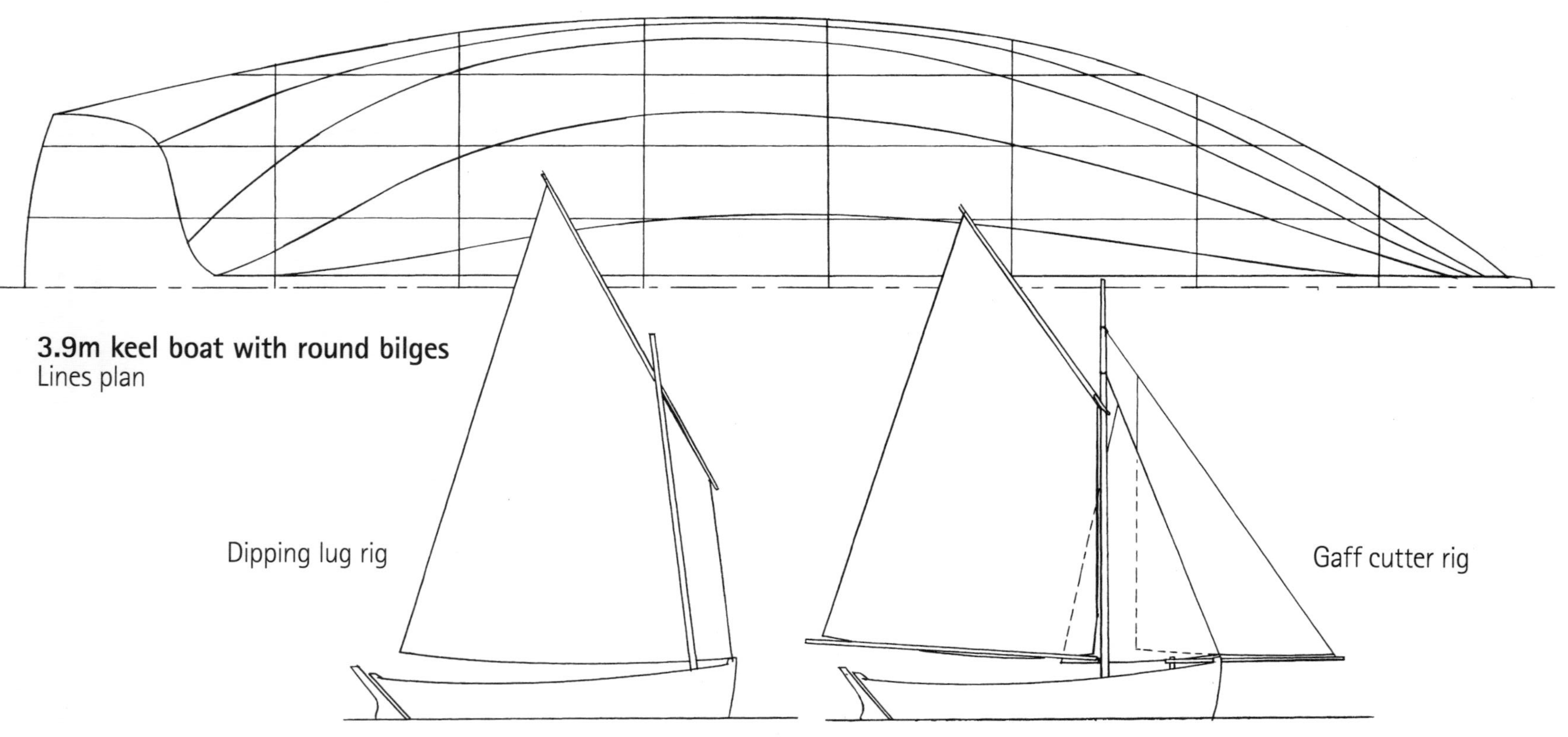

3.9m keel boat with round bilges
Lines plan

3.9m keelboat with round bilges

Construction plan

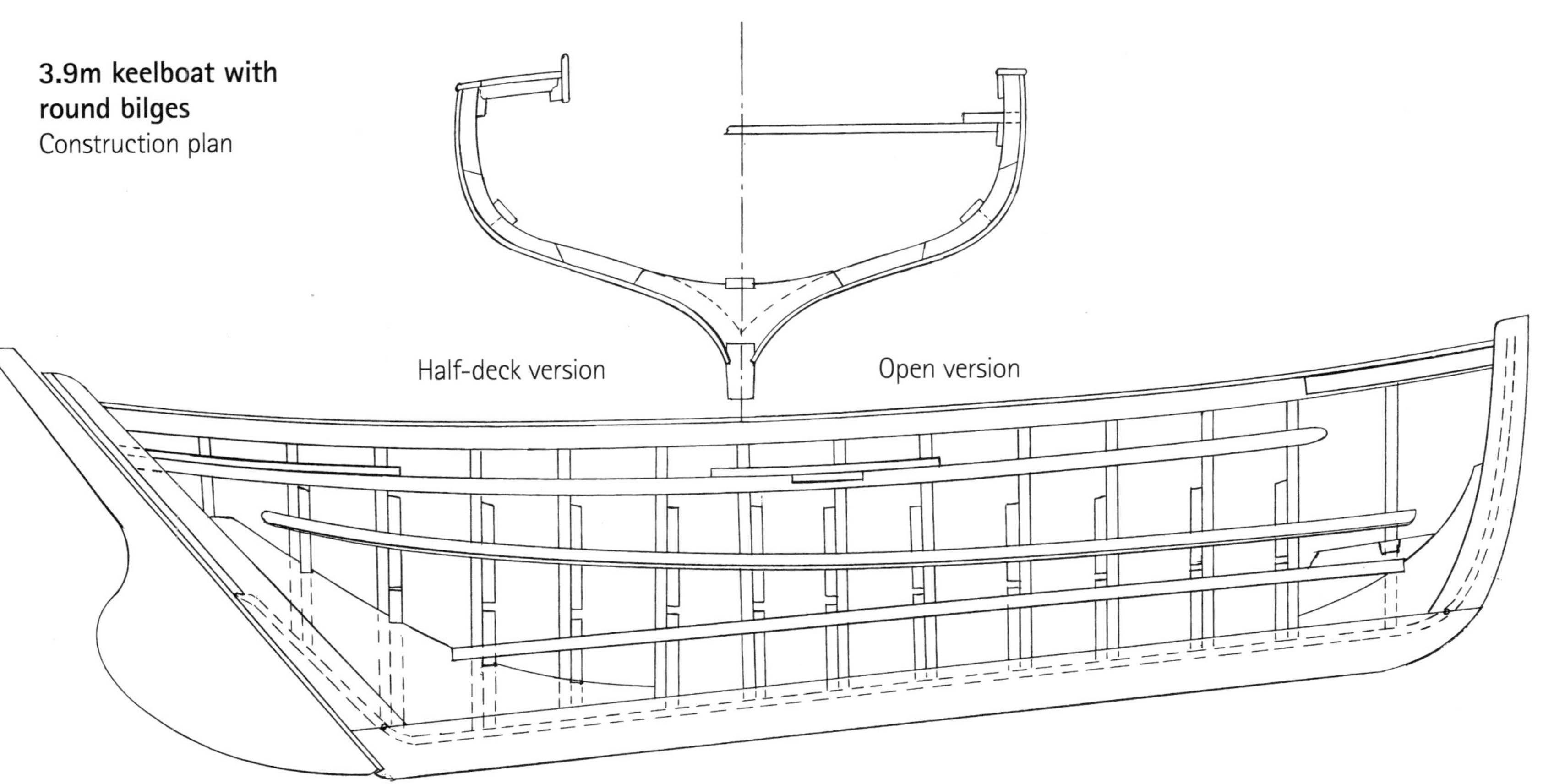

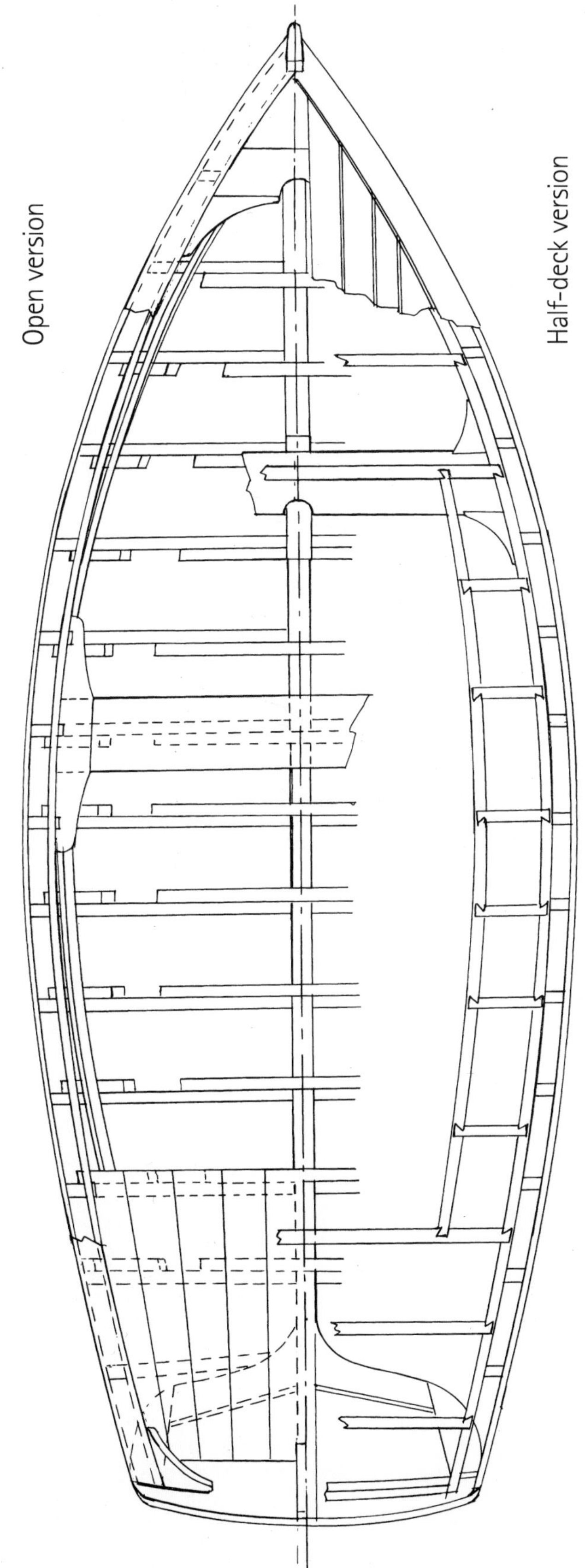
Open version
Half-deck version

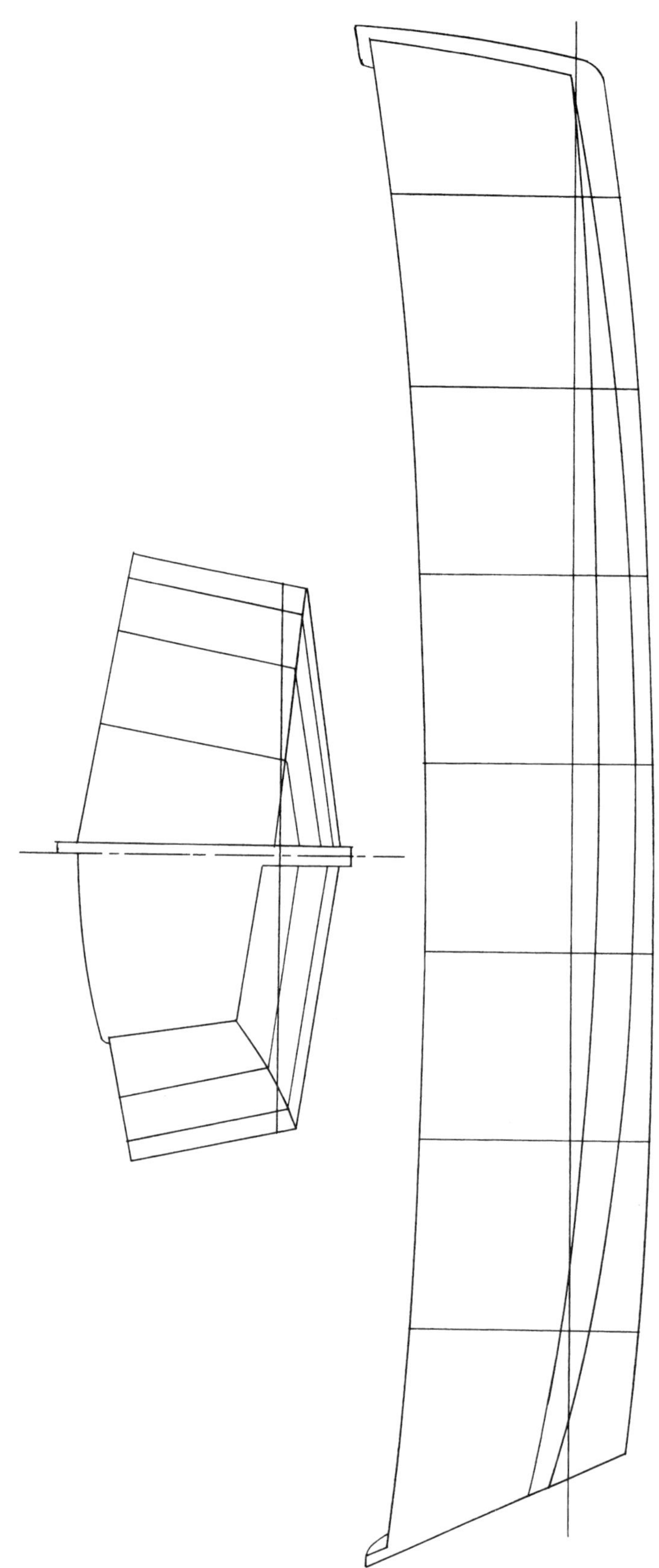

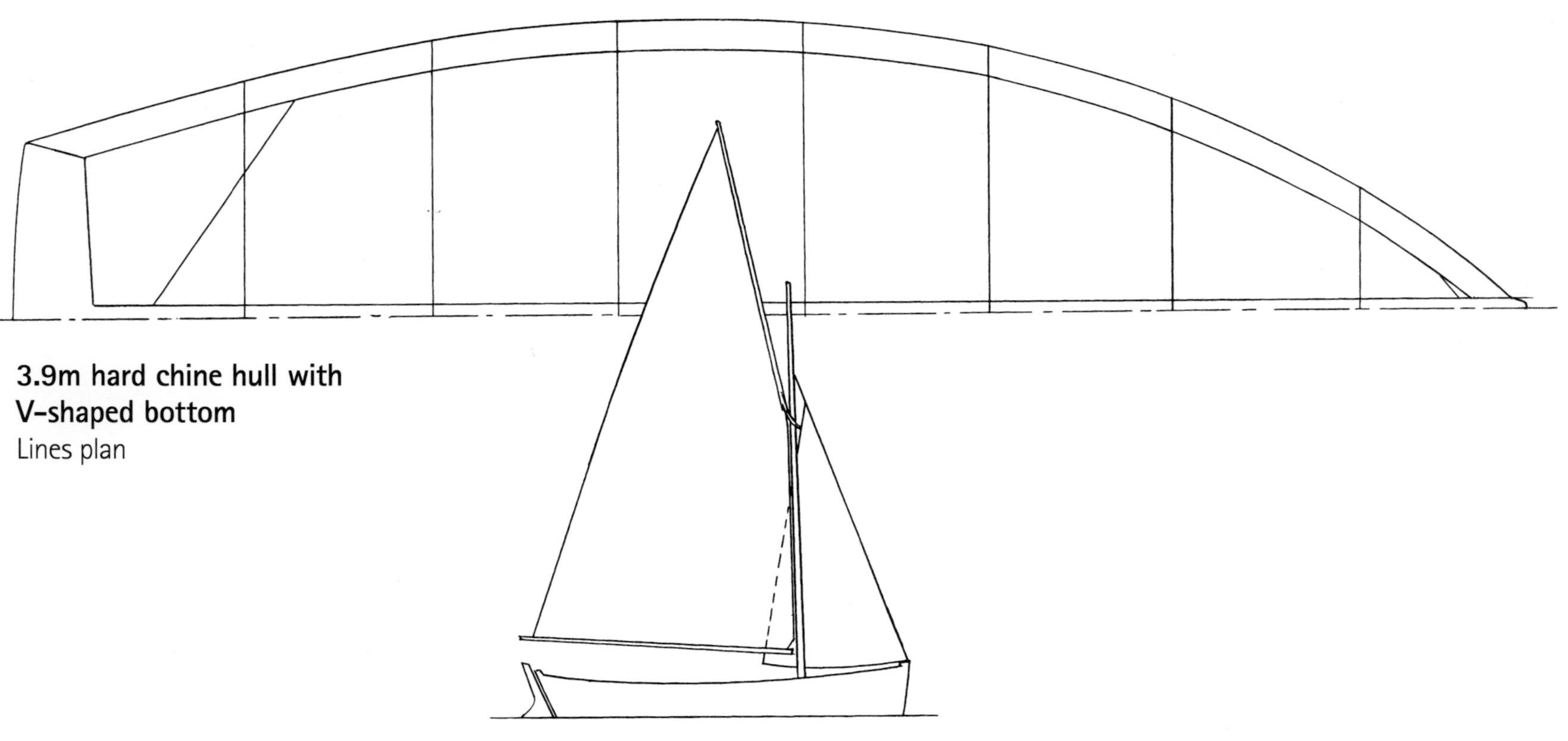

3.9m hard chine hull with V-shaped bottom
Lines plan

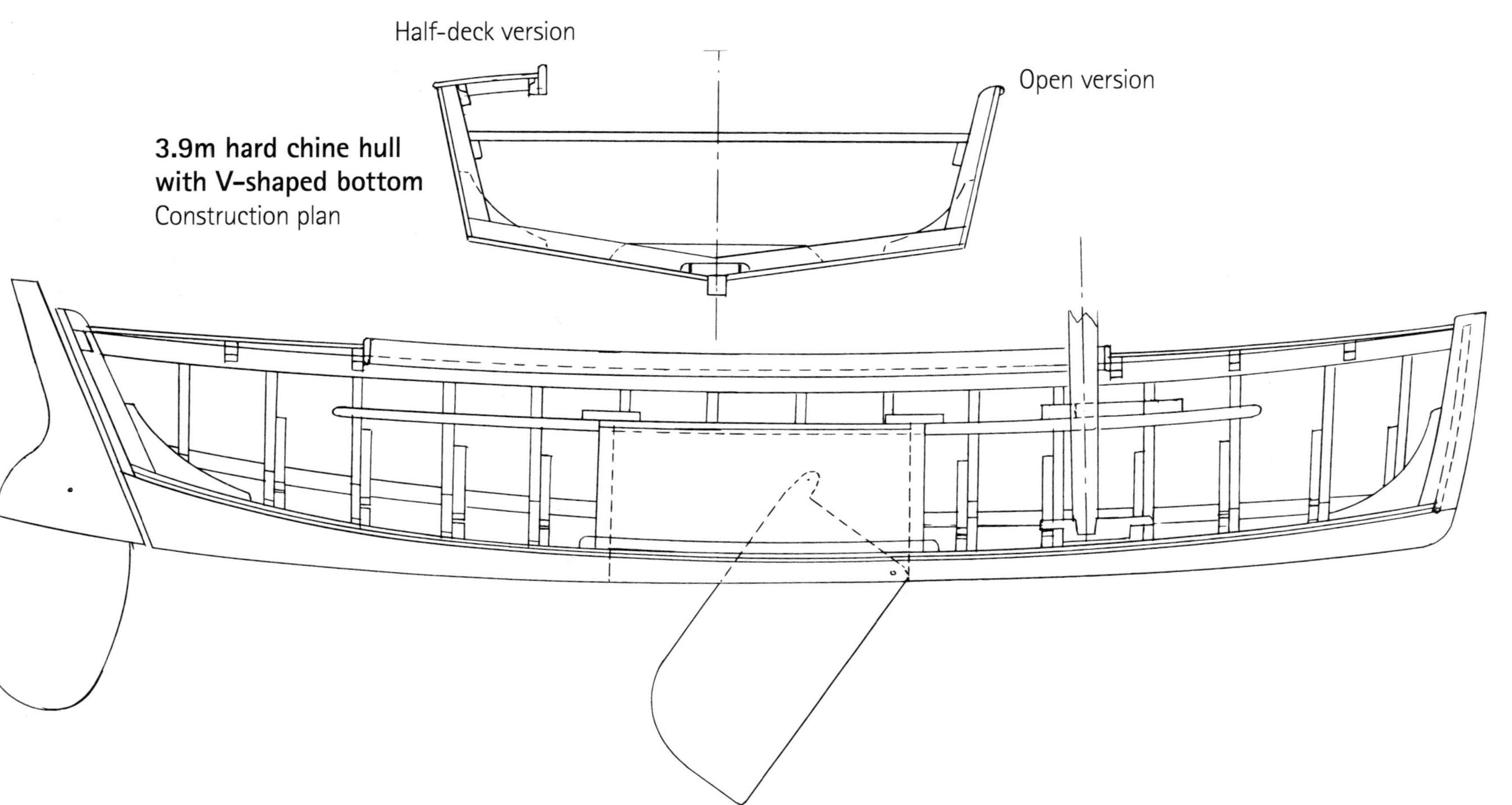

3.9m hard chine hull with V-shaped bottom
Construction plan

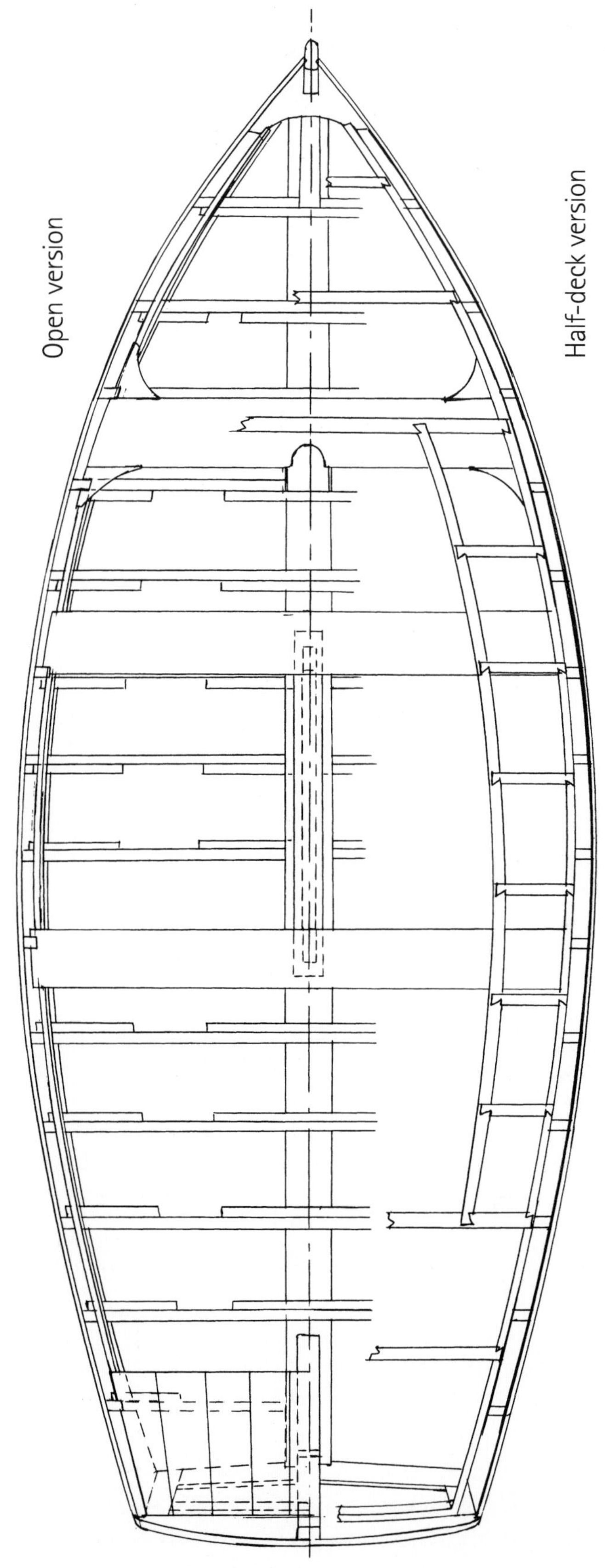
Open version
Half-deck version

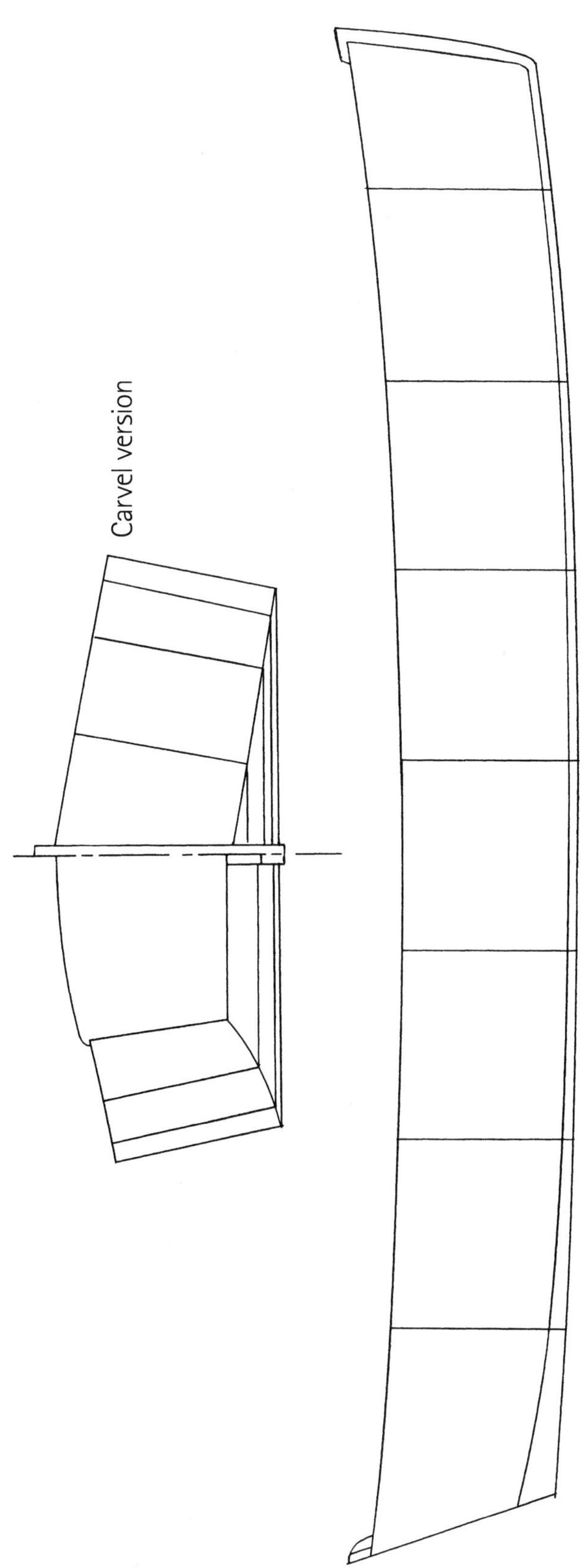
Carvel version

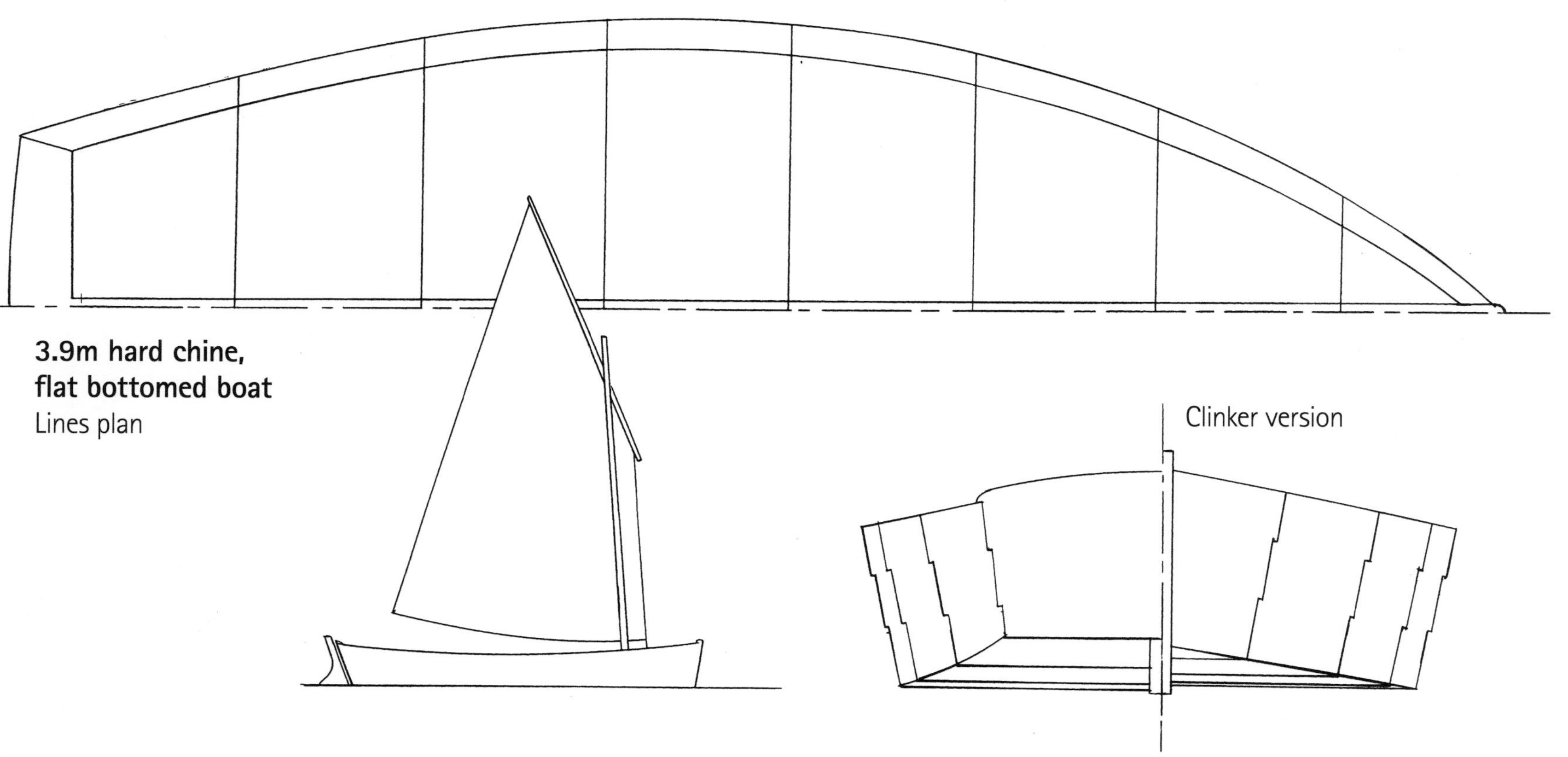

3.9m hard chine, flat bottomed boat
Lines plan

3.9m hard chine, flat bottomed boat
Construction plan

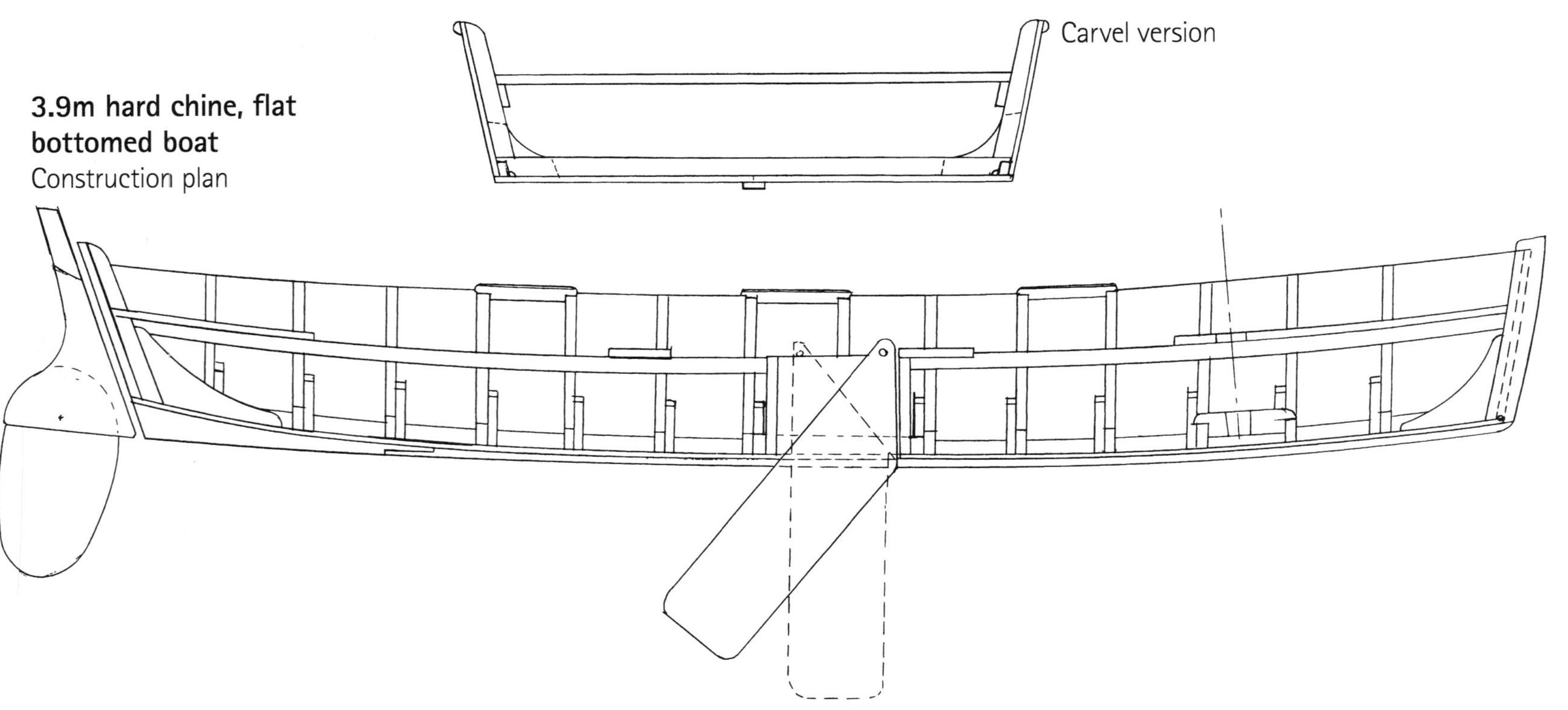

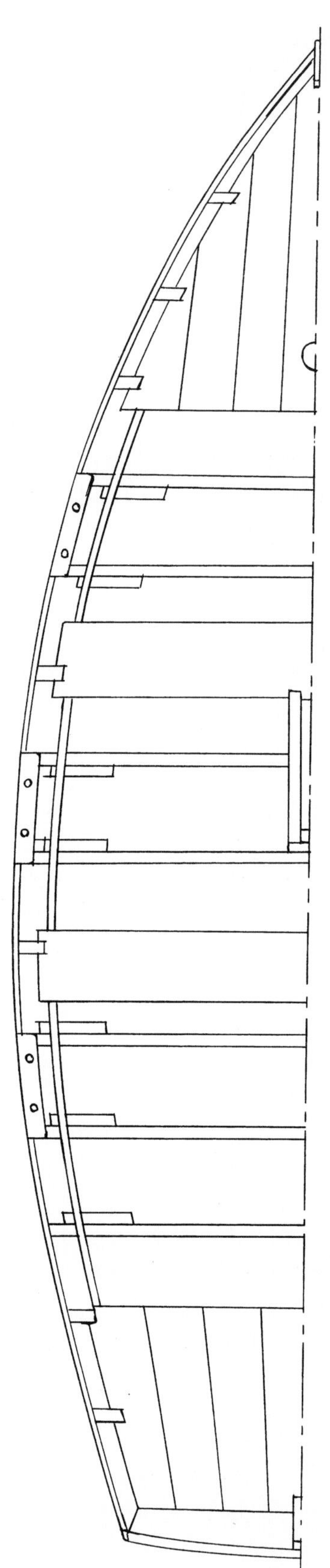

Clinker version

HOW DO YOU DRAW INSPIRATION FROM A PLAN?

If you take the example of the round bilge dinghy (**figure 1**), her length/beam ratio would make her a rather comfortable, versatile boat. There is nothing to prevent you from extending her a little as in **figure 2**; all you have to do is to space the frame timbers further apart, which is something some yards don't think twice about doing with their moulds. This gives her the average proportions of a traditional working boat.

If we wish a dinghy to be even longer, say 5m or more, the beam and probably the depth as well, must also be increased. However, it should be noted that the length/beam ratio isn't constant. A large boat is relatively narrow in comparison with a small one; in other words, a small boat requires a larger relative beam for stability.

Again you need to think about how the boat is going to be used. If she will be used solely for rowing in calm waters, she may be lengthened, as she has been in **figure 3**. If we wish to build a boat fitted with a centreboard, in the style of a small yacht, the boat may be widened and flattened as in **figure 4**. Her looks are reminiscent of a 'clipper' with a centreboard from the very first days of yachting on the River Seine!

These calculations should be approached very carefully. It is impossible to design a 12m boat by multiplying the sides of a 4m dinghy by 3!

A lot of other examples will be found in journals, old books and in the vast array of articles in the French traditional boat magazine *Chasse-Marée* or *Classic Boat* (UK) and *WoodenBoat* (USA). Traditional boats on the water, modern replicas or old restored boats, should be closely studied to understand their construction and the method of assembly. Observing these carefully is an indispensable prerequisite for setting about a construction project.

You should, however, be both cautious and modest in your ambitions: for the design, choose a boat type with recognised seagoing qualities, which really suits the intended use. Furthermore, don't make anything other than minor modifications if they appear to create an 'improvement' and, if in doubt, get the alteration checked by a designer. In any case, the amateur builder shouldn't forget that the current Recreational Craft Directive (RCD) concerns them in the same way as it does professional builders. The new directives have the merit of making each person face up to their responsibilities: no plan can be used and no boat can be built without first having tested it using various calculations, the essential qualities of the boat's behaviour at sea (mainly via stability and buoyancy calculations), and having adhered to a suitable construction standard (see the regulations in the Practical Information on page 107).

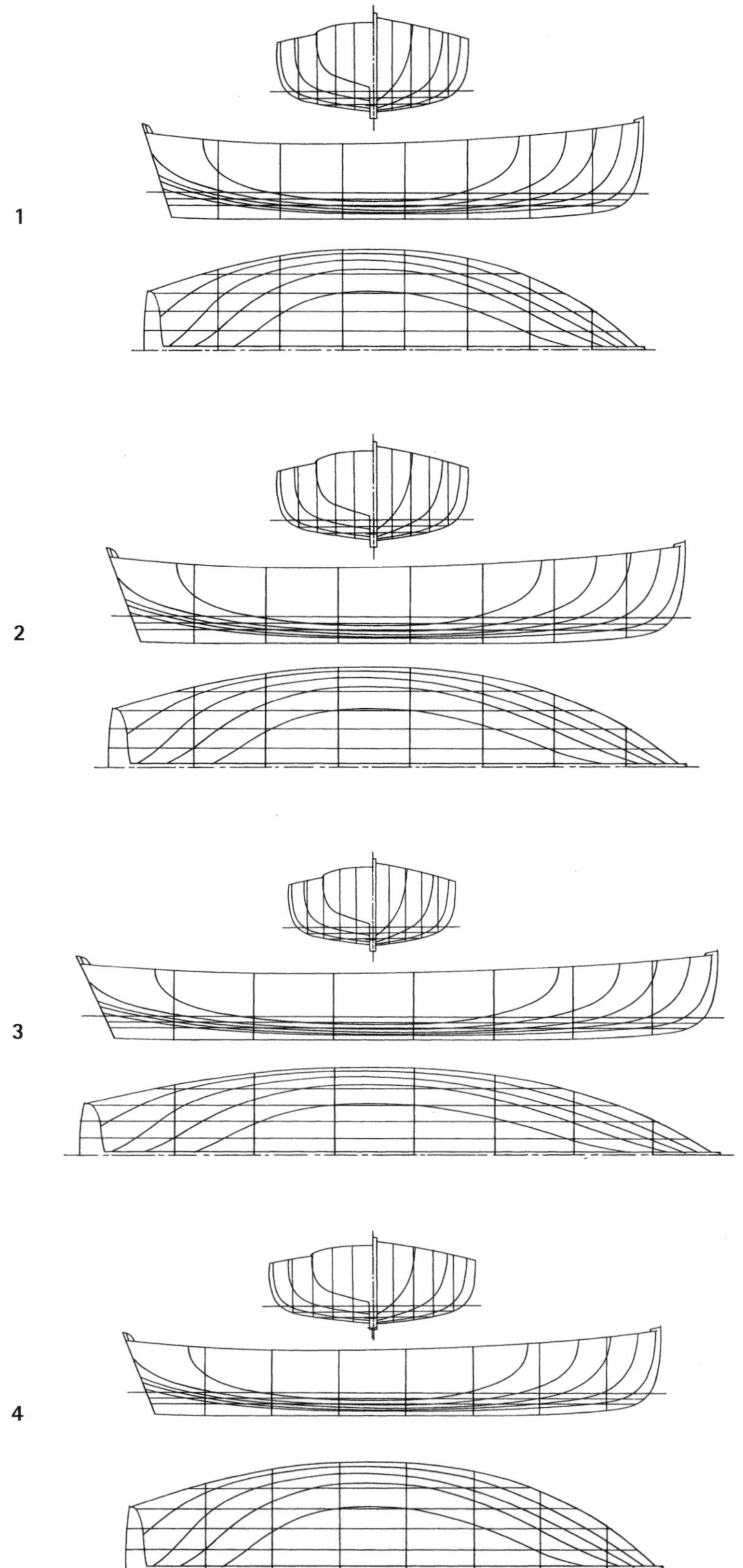
1
2
3
4

TAKING OFF LINES

In certain cases you will choose to take the lines off an old boat whose plans no longer exist or have never existed. In this instance it's the boat herself that serves as the model for drawing plans and constructing a new, identical craft.

Prior to undertaking such an operation, it is still necessary to ensure that the boat is worth the effort. Has she been built by a good yard? Has her design proved satisfactory? Has it been modified over the years to such an extent that it no longer resembles the original shape? Is she really a representative example of her type? It's worthwhile investigating all such matters.

Taking the lines off an existing boat consists of measuring the hull extremely accurately. This operation, which requires little equipment, is within everyone's capability, provided it is carried out with method and precision. The main requirement is the ability to work around the boat, which should be aground on a bank or slipway and positioned perfectly upright. First, we try to draw the boat's profile by measuring the length of her keel, the height of the bow and that of the transom, and by taking a few intermediate measurements, for example along the sheerline (the curve of the gunwale running from bow to stern).

On this profile we draw the positions of the transverse sections destined for the sectional plan. Three sections form a minimum, but five are desirable and more are even better; their positions can be marked on the hull by a chalk line. The measurements at these stations are then taken directly from the hull surface, with the help of one or two divided scales placed vertically and horizontally, initially pinpointing the key points: rabbet line, sheer line, then the intermediate stations distributed along the hull.

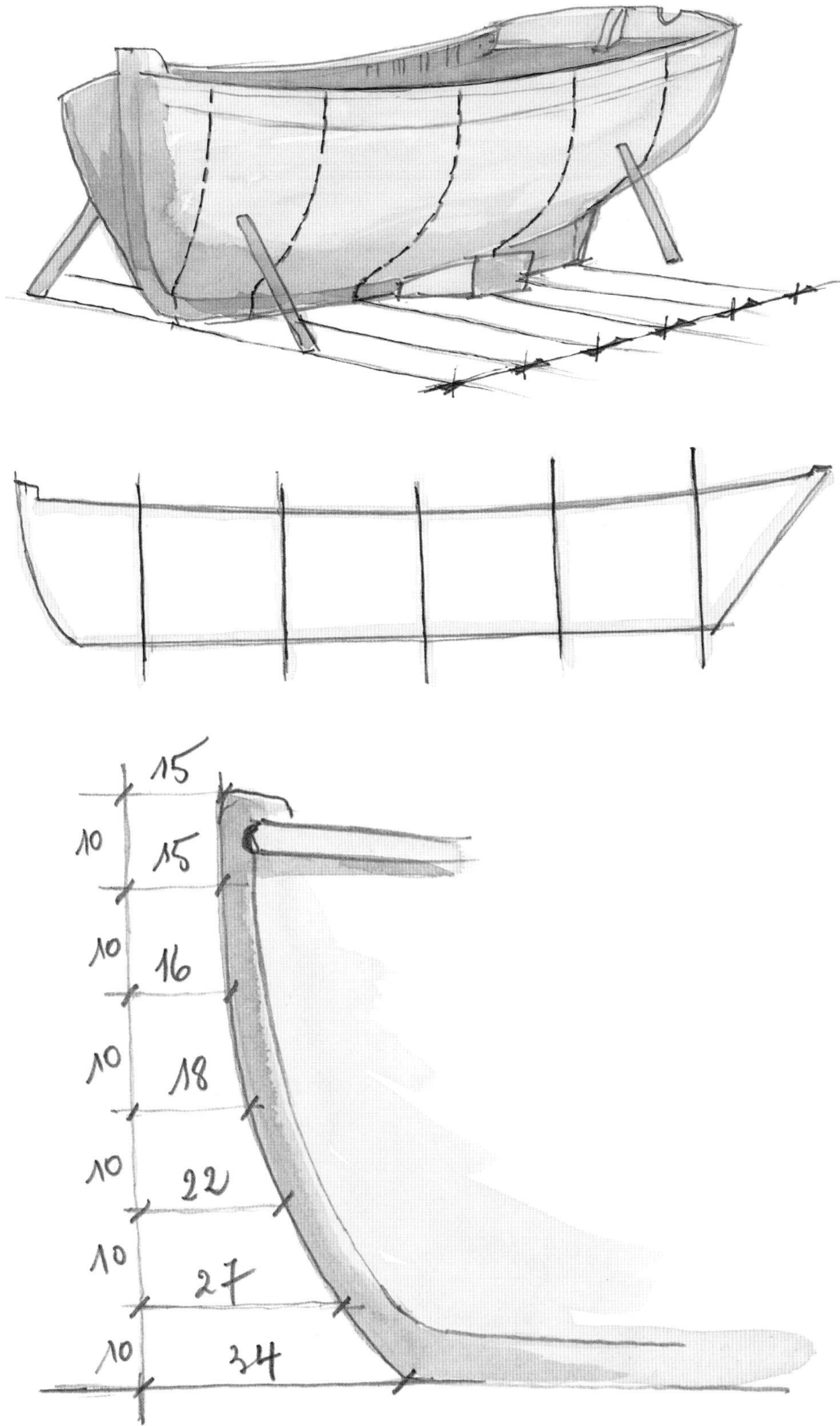
15
10
15
10
16
10
18
10
22
10
27
10
34

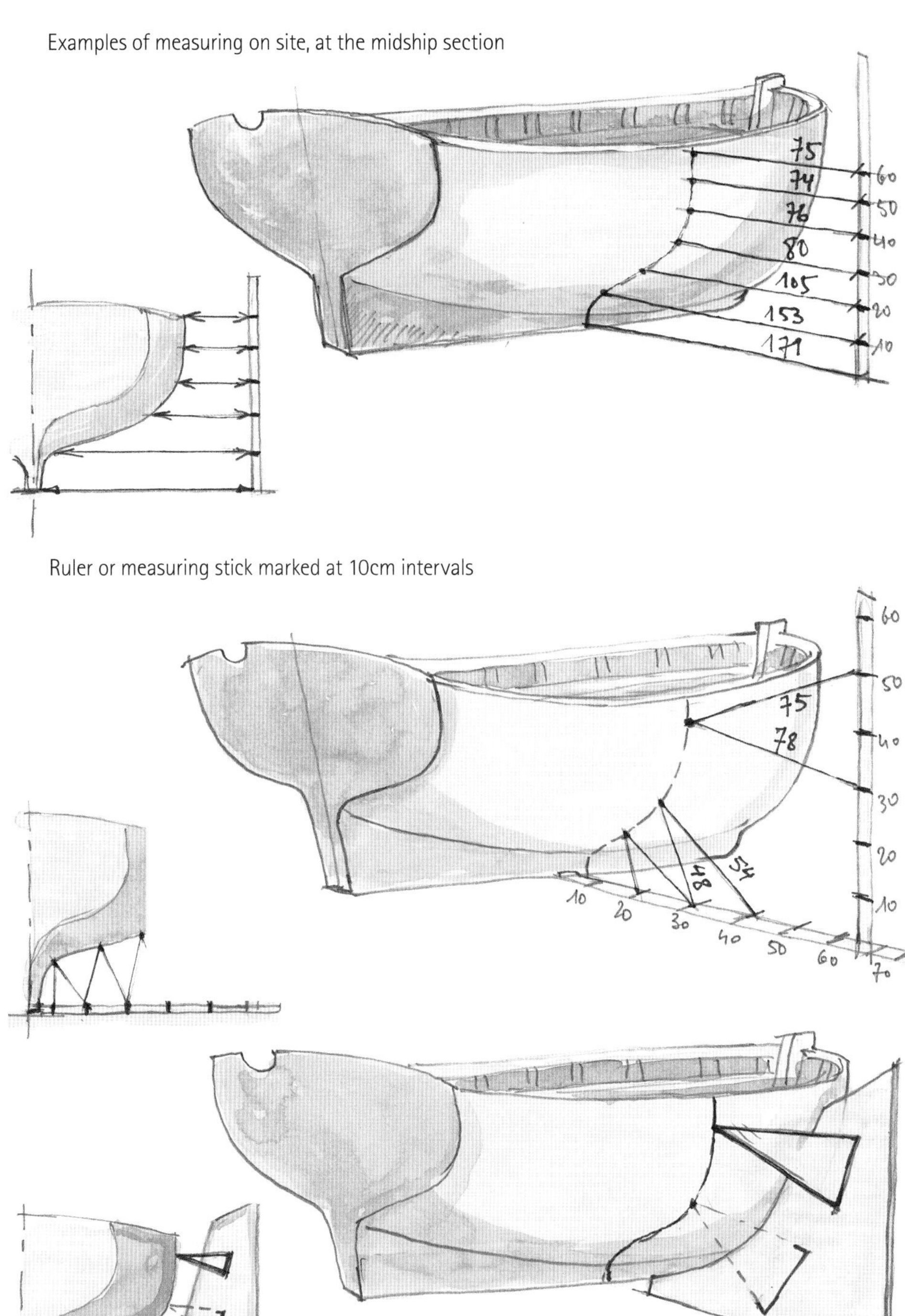

Examples of measuring on site, at the midship section

Ruler or measuring stick marked at 10cm intervals

For this, various methods can be used, as the illustrations show. You can use Cartesian coordinates or polar coordinates, or by the use of a large square ticked off all along the section line, whose base is marked on a provisional template with approximately the exterior shape of the hull (you can also use a special rule).

Even though it is possible to undertake the full scale lofting from these lines measurements (page 37), it is always preferable to draw up a plan and even to check it with the help of a half model (page 36).

All the dimensions taken from the hull, which serves as a model, will be reduced to the scale of the plan. To be able to plot the latter, we choose a simple scale enabling us to avoid calculation errors: for example 1:10, a centimetre becoming 1 millimetre, or 1:5 where 1cm on the hull becomes 2mm on the plan.

DRAWING THE LINES PLAN FROM MEASUREMENTS

We begin with the transverse sections plan (body plan) from five stations along the hull with the right-hand side of the plan representing the hull shape viewed from ahead, and the left-hand side the shape viewed from astern. This transverse sections plan comes directly from the measurements of the hull and includes all the inaccuracies due to working in the field. It is essential to check it and to 'fair' it by plotting the horizontal and then the vertical sections (the diagonal curves at times too).

The measurements are taken from the boat's centreline out to the hull at each station, along one of the chosen horizontal planes (waterlines), number III for example. These measurements enable you to plot waterline number III.

While drawing our plan view we see that, for example, point B falls outside a smoothly curved line and point C is too far inside it. To fair the lines up, we move these two points and correct the lines with the new B' and C' points on the plan. The movement of these points results in a faired curve at stations 2 and 3. Waterlines I, II, III, IV are similarly plotted and, if necessary, faired, enabling us to gradually refine the shape of the transverse curves.

The plotting of these longitudinal curves enables you to check the other hull planes and shapes. Here again, alterations will be necessary before the shape of the hull is completed and each point measured is located in exactly the right position in the three views to give a fair hull.

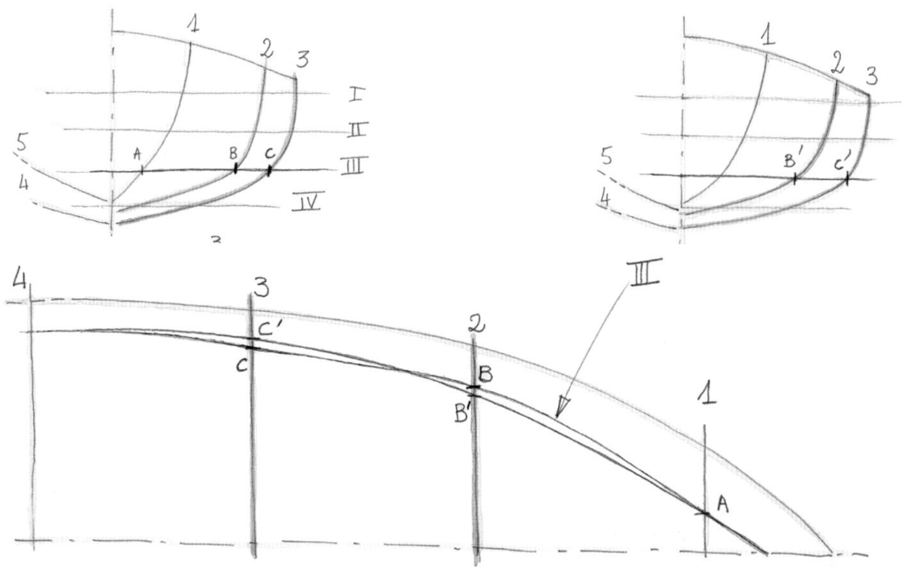

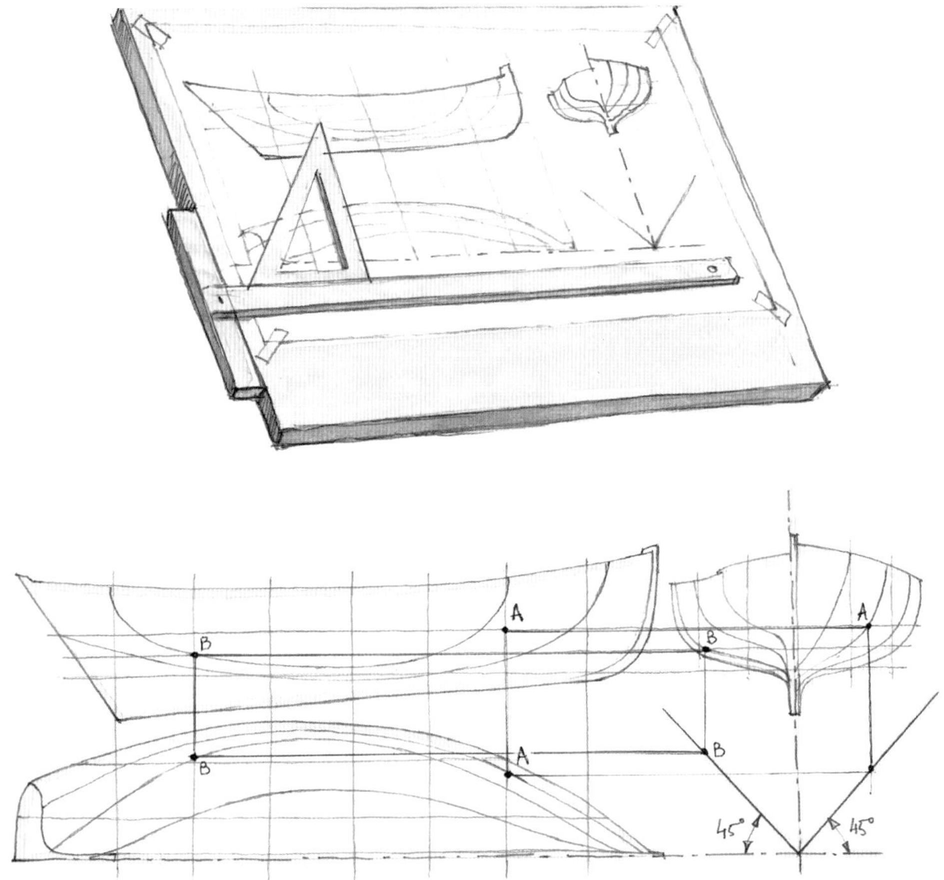

Note the use of two 45 degree lines on the drawings, enabling the points to be referenced from one view to another, by working with a T and a set square on a drawing board.

This modest equipment, to which we add a little grey matter, enables us to plot just as good a plan, albeit less quickly, as a piece of 3D design software. For some time yet, the drawing board will remain the easiest and most economical way for amateurs to create a set of plans.

It is advisable to work on and fair the boat's hull lines as many times as necessary, in order to obtain the level of accuracy that will make building easier. This 'virtual' stage must be conducted until you reach a point where you are entirely satisfied. Don't forget that a misplaced dimension on the plan, or a curve that is drawn badly, will result in inaccuracies that are even trickier to rectify once they're carved out in good oak than when they are a simple pencil line on paper.

Nevertheless, it does take a certain amount of time before this geometry is properly mastered. It's good practice to draw imaginary plans, which aren't intended for construction, as often as possible and for pleasure.

Now the plan exists and it is time to redraw it on a scale of 1:1 (full size) in a process known as 'lofting', in order to make the moulds and begin the construction. However, this phase of the full scale lofting is greatly assisted if it's preceded by making a half model, which will enable the hull shape to be visualised better.

MAKING A HALF MODEL

The half model, as the name suggests, is a scale model of half the hull* (port or starboard). It is made by cutting pieces of wood to the shape of each waterline one side of the centreline, the thickness of each being the separation between the waterlines on the profile plan. These shaped pieces of wood are then screwed and/or glued together in the correct order, the position of one of the sections having been marked on the centreline edge to facilitate accurate alignment. The surplus timber is then removed down to the edge of each waterline taking care that not too much is removed.

The half model thus produced should be an exact reproduction of the plan. If, after examined it, the shape seems to be appropriate, that means that plans are also satisfactory. If it appears to be too full anywhere, more wood can be taken off to achieve the desired shape. On the other hand, if it appears too fine anywhere it will be necessary to modify the plans accordingly and, perhaps, make a second half model.

In the case described here, where the lines are based on an existing hull, it will be easy to compare the original and the model, and the least one can hope for is that they resemble each other closely.

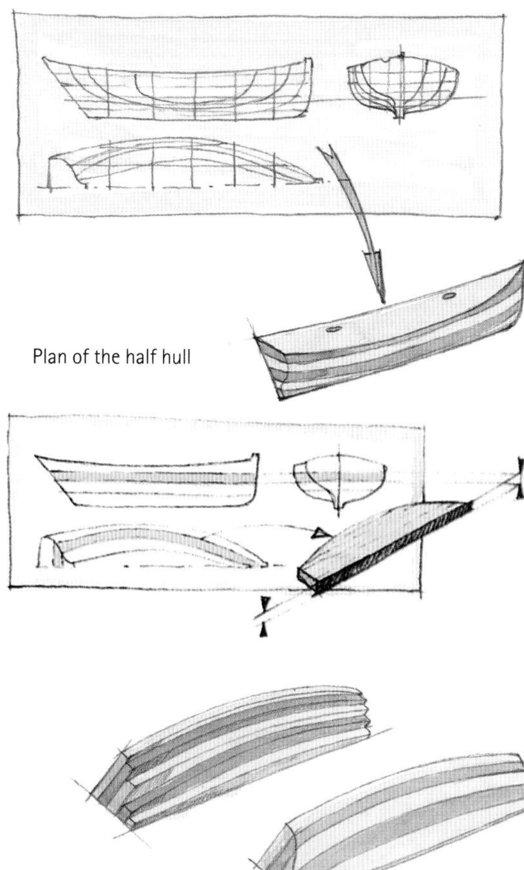

Plan of the half hull

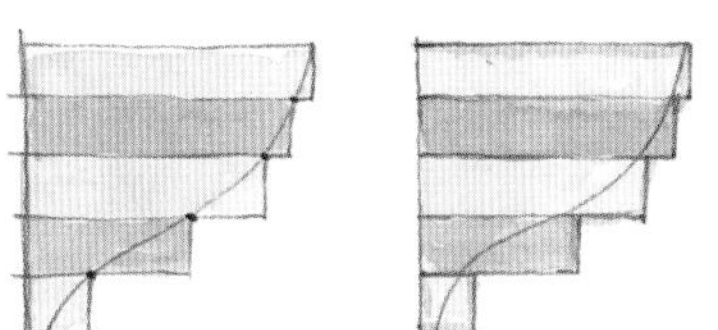

*By only making half the hull, the other half comprising exactly the same information, we avoid the risk of asymmetry.

THE TRADITIONAL HALF MODEL

The use of the half model as a means of checking a plan is not a modern idea. The half model carved by a boatbuilder was made to develop a boat's shape directly, in collaboration with his/her backer, without drawing plans. The boatbuilder stacked the small wooden boards and pegged them together until they formed a block, which he then sculpted to create the shape of the boat. He drew her profile on one side of the block, on the ends he drew her half-section at maximum beam, and on the top of the block he drew her shape in plan view. The hull shape was then roughly outlined by sculpting it directly into the block and refined, little by little, until a hull shape was obtained that satisfied both the boatbuilder and his client. All that remained then was to pull out the pegs to obtain the curves of the horizontal waterlines and to transfer the transverse sections at set stations onto small boards that could be scaled up to form templates for the frame timbers.

For the amateur it is best to limit oneself to the very traditional shapes and, in principle, exclude the creation or design of a boat without reference to a known model. Apprentice designers are often confronted, as is the case for apprentice witches and wizards, with the worst disappointments.

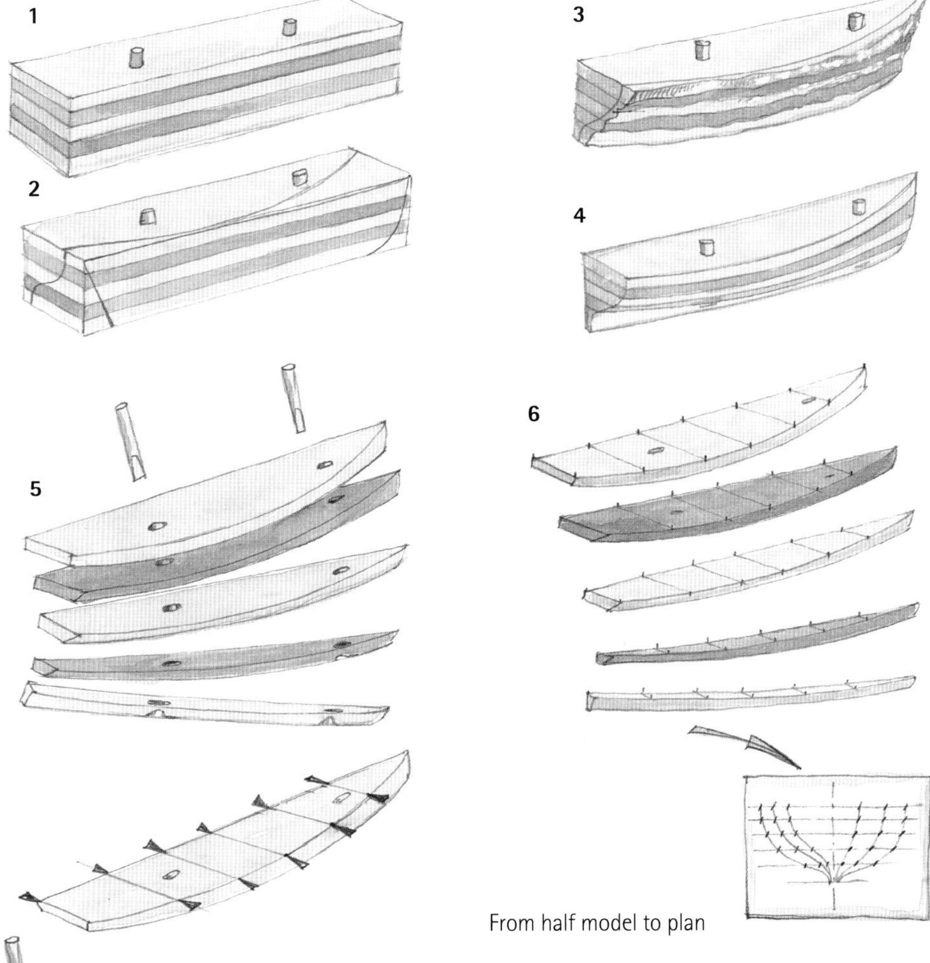

From half model to plan

LOFTING

The lines plans and the half model are small scale; the operation of full scale lofting consists of reproducing the plans at actual (full) size. If the plan is 1:10, the most practical scale, each millimetre on paper will become 10mm at full size. If the scale is 1:5, which is often the case, each millimetre on the plan represents five millimetres when enlarged to full scale, which is five times the dimensions measured on the plan.

Lofting is carried out on the floor, on a very smooth surface, for example on sheets of thin plywood, placed edge to edge and painted white. The lofting is done in pencil and consists of reproducing the three views of the drawn plans. At this full scale you obtain a plan that is much more precise than the scaled down version. Any imperfections can still be corrected at this stage and the fairing of each line or section will enable you to put the finishing touches to the whole thing.

The purpose of this plan with the three planes - sections, buttocks and waterlines - is to obtain a perfect and fair representation of the hull shape, which is essential when making a framework from sawn frames. However, in the case of a construction with moulds, the full scale lofting of transverse sections will be sufficient (fairing will be done later with the help of temporary battens offered up to the moulds).

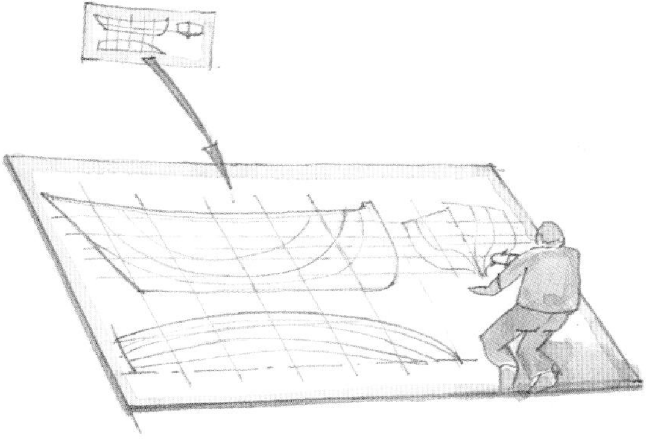

Lofting the plans full size

TABLE OF OFFSETS

This table of measurements is attached to the plans. It relates to the body plan and shows the distance from the centreline of the point at which each waterline (the horizontal plane parallel to the designed waterline) meets each station - the 'half breadth' of the hull at that height and that fore and aft position. In the drawing, the half breadth of waterline II at station 3 is 72cm. Easy to consult, the table of offsets avoids repeated measurement of the full scale plan.

The table of offsets is usually supplied by the designer, who has created it after fairing onto a full scale lofting or via 'digital fairing' in a computer program. The accuracy of this latter technique is sufficient to enable the lofting of transverse sections directly onto the moulds.

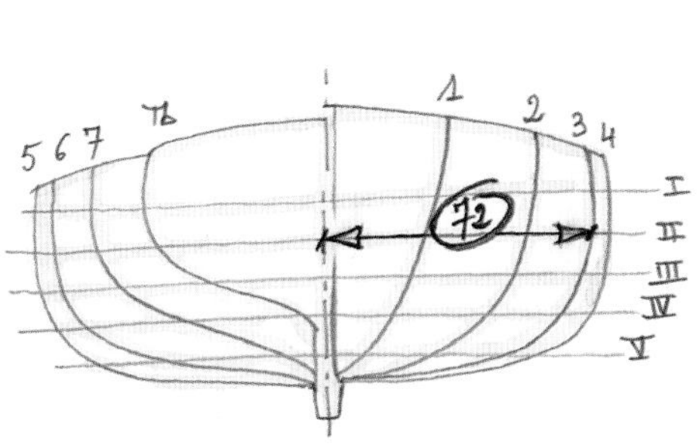

	1	2	3	4	5	6	7	Tb
I	31	56	73	78	79	74	63	49
II	27	55	72	77	78	73	61	44
III	23	51	70	76	77	71	54	28
IV	19	45	64	72	73	65	36	5
V	11	30	51	58	60	41	10	4

LOFTING FOR PLANKING, LOFTING FOR FRAMES

The lines plan shows the outer line of the boat's hull; that's to say the external surface of the hull. To construct the component parts and, in particular, her ribs, you must determine the hull shape (dimensions) after deducting the thickness of the planking or skin. The interior lines correspond to both the internal surface of the

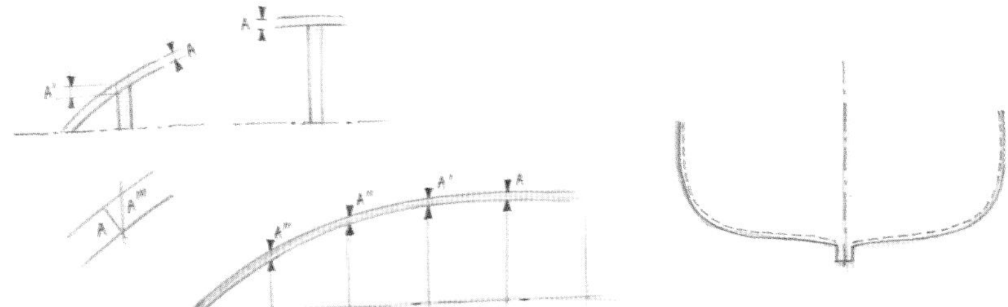

hull planking and the external surface of the ribs or frames, which lie against each other. The simplest method for lofting the frames, from the lofting for the outside of the hull planking, is to draw a new curve parallel to the first, inset by the thickness of the planking or skin. We will use this method, but need to be aware that it is only accurate in the midship section. For greater precision you must take into account the angle that the hull planking makes to the centreline, which increases the further forward or aft you get from the midship section.

A' is equal to A, because the hull planking is perpendicular to line 3 (or parallel at this point to the boat's centreline). A'' is greater than A, because the hull planking runs at an angle. A''' is even larger than A, because the hull planking is angled more obliquely.

Not taking into account the variation between the outside of the planking and the lofted frames would lead to a slight increase in the shape at the fore and aft sections of the boat. For a dinghy, this difference would not be more than a few millimetres and makes this work unnecessary. Some lines plans are drawn directly without a frame and hence the deduction no longer needs to be made; this is the case for the three plans used as examples in this book.

CONSTRUCTION PLANS

The lines plans previously studied only give the shape, without any indication of the construction method. The construction plan provides the shape of the timbers necessary for construction of the boat: shape, assembly method, size. This plan is often completed by annotations relating to the scantlings of secondary parts, the species of wood to use and the size of the rivets or nails used.

In the case of making a replica of an existing boat, all the information relating to the frame must be transferred from the original boat. It is sufficient to go and see her and to look closely at the construction details. However, it will be useful to make a construction plan from the boat, to avoid making too many trips, so we will look next at the assembly methods and the sections of each part. Nevertheless, however much care goes into the plan, having the original boat nearby will be a precious aid during the construction phase. If this isn't possible, a large amount of very detailed photographic work can make up for the lack of a model close to the workshop.

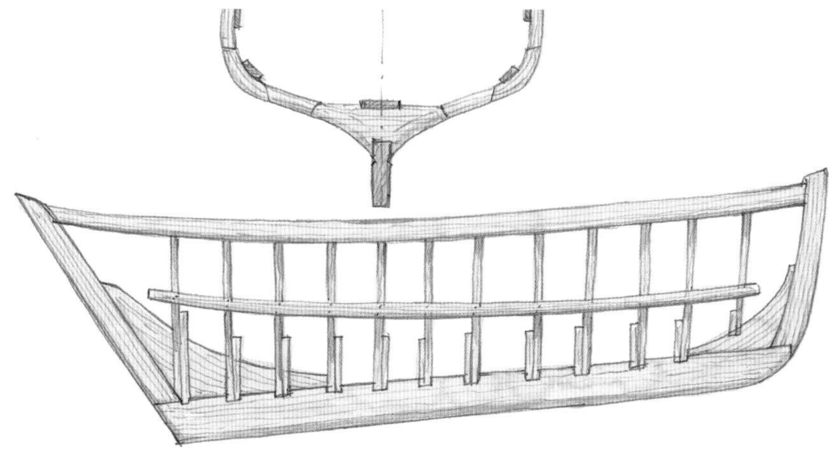

PROFILE AND MIDSHIP SECTION ALONE

Occasionally, a full set of lines hasn't been drawn, either because the boat serving as a model has distorted too much, or the plans are too basic. In this situation, the simple profile of the hull and the lines from the midship section are sufficient to undertake the construction using light stringers to give the hull shape. It means that the boat's final lines are developed during construction, a method that was widely used in small yards.

First the longitudinal centreline structure (see the following pages) is built according to the hull profile. Then a temporary mould of the midship section is offered up on the backbone and a set of light stringers are attached to simulate the planking of the hull and hence its lines. With these in place the hull shape can be seen (and adjusted) and the measurements of the missing frames fore and aft from the midship section determined at each required station.

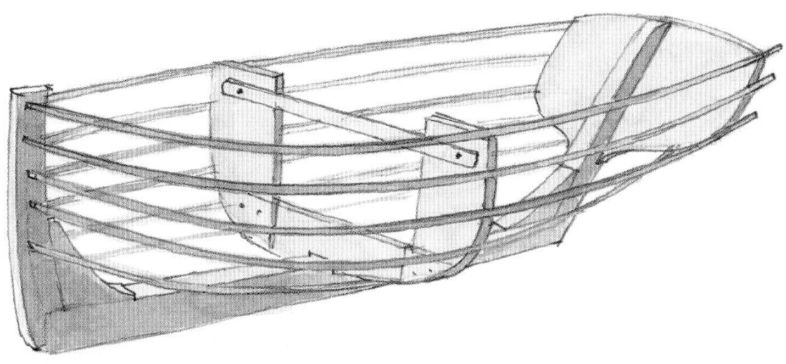

TRADITIONAL CONSTRUCTION

To construct a traditional boat, you need wood, a few tools and the skill of a builder who knows how to fashion and assemble the parts forming the framework.

While different boatbuilders develop their own specific building methods and features which give their individuality, the basic construction methods are common to all.

These basic ideas are explained here, from positioning the keel to the finishing touches to the hull.

BOATBUILDING TIMBERS

Timber used in boatbuilding is chosen according to the characteristics of its species – hardness, density, flexibility, resistance to rot – as well as the shapes of the tree, or part of the tree, which will provide straight or curved sections of wood, according to needs. Finally, each tree can have flaws or diseases that you have to know how to recognise.

HARDWOODS

These are principally broad-leaved trees from European forests. Oak is the most widely used of these. It's used for curved sawn ribs, as straight timbers for the keel, bent ribs and possibly as hull planking. You can construct a boat entirely of oak and, though she'll be heavy, she'll be very strong. Elm was often used beneath the waterline (though it rots in freshwater), but since the devastation caused by Dutch Elm disease you seldom find it anymore. Acacia is frequently used for bent or steamed ribs; you can also use ash and oak.

CONIFEROUS WOODS

Softer but more flexible and lighter than the broad-leaved trees, conifers, thanks to their high resin content, stand up to exposure to weather. We use them a great deal for masts, spars and also for hull planking, sometimes even for the construction of modest dinghies. Pitch pine is an often used and excellent wood for hull planking. Larch and Oregon pine (or Douglas fir) are used for hull planking as well as for masts and spars. Scots pine (Northern pine, Scotch fir) is used for masts and spars, because it's very light, as is Norwegian spruce.

Selecting naturally grown shapes for structural parts is quite an art

TROPICAL HARDWOODS

Used in yachts rather than working craft, they were initially selected for their beauty when varnished. Some of them are also of high quality and resistant to rot. Mahogany is well suited to the planking of yacht hulls and for the construction of their accommodation. So too is sapele. We also make frames from African mahogany, niangon and iroko.

FLAWS AND DISEASES IN WOOD

The main flaws in wood are knots – especially if they are numerous and likely to come out – deep fissures and splits, also cracking due to frost.

Diseases are caused by a microscopic fungus whose filaments – mycelium – cause a decomposition of the wood referred to as dry rot. The parts affected are of no use and can contaminate others. Wet rot occurs when the wood is enclosed in poorly ventilated sections of the boat. Rainwater accelerates wet rot, whilst saltwater slows the process. Rotten timbers must be removed as soon as possible if they are large, otherwise they should be treated with specialised products.

THE MAIN FRAME TIMBERS

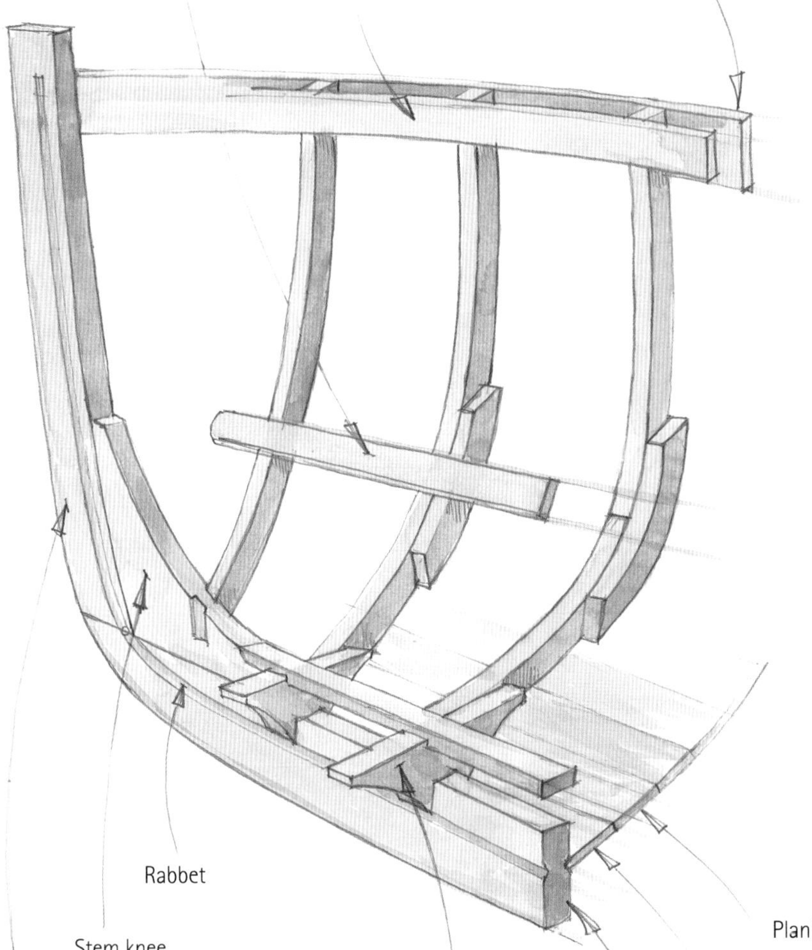

Sheer strake (or gunwale)

Bilge stringer

Inwale

Rabbet

Stem knee

Stem

Floor

Planking

Garboard strake

Keel

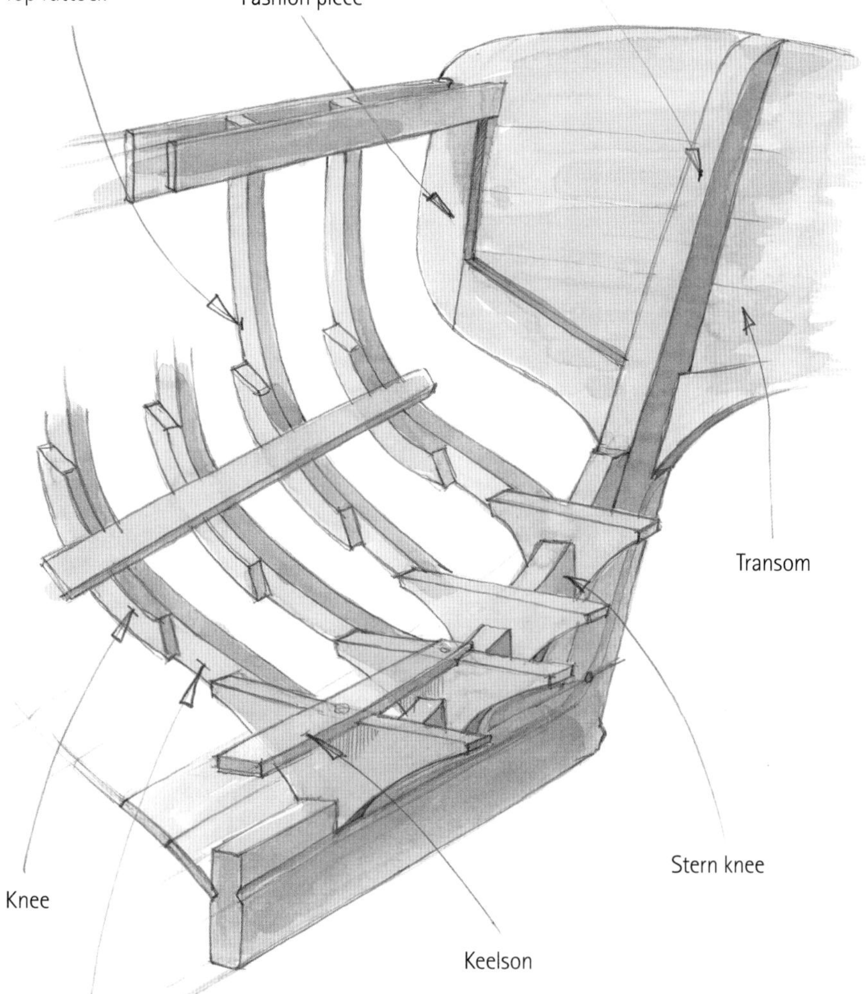

Stern post

Top futtock

Fashion piece

Transom

Stern knee

Knee

Keelson

Keel futtock

THE LONGITUDINAL CENTRELINE STRUCTURE

This longitudinal centreline structure is the boat's real backbone and the point from which construction generally begins.

KEEL, STEM, STERN POST, STEM AND STERN KNEES

It is made up of three parts: the roughly horizontal keel, on which the stem is attached to the forward section and the stern post to the aft section. These three parts alone provide an outline of the boat's eventual shape.

The stem and stern posts are joined to the keel with the help of mortise and tenon joints or halving joints and then pegged. To strengthen the assembly, two curved timbers known as the stem and stern knees, are added to the joint: the forward stem knee between the stem and the keel, the aft stern knee between the stern post and the keel. With these five parts, the longitudinal centreline structure of small dinghies is complete.

The keel is often doubled in thickness, either by adding a hog, which caps it, or a keelson, which is a longitudinal timber placed inside the boat to reinforce the keel, to which it is fastened. The floors are inserted between the keel and keelson and are joining pieces between the backbone of the hull and its transverse frames and ribs. A rabbet (or rebate) is cut out along the length of the keel to form the joint between the keel and the hull planking.

For the frames we use hardwoods like oak or certain tropical hardwoods, such as iroko.

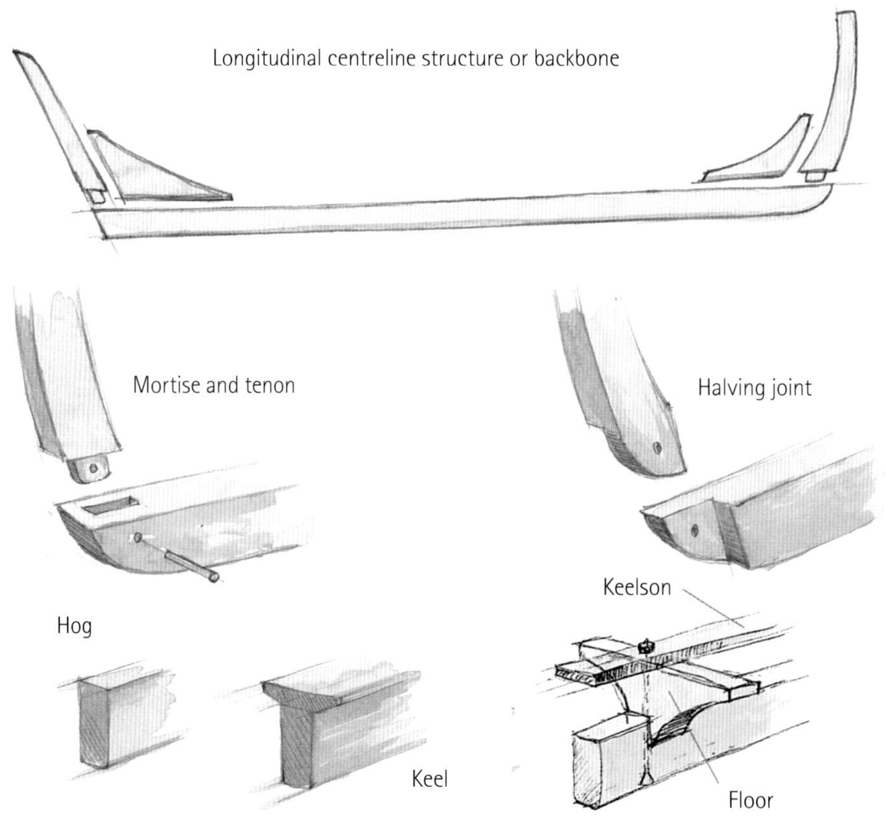

On boats with a deep draught, whose large keel area or lateral plane resists leeway under sail, the keel is reinforced inside the boat by laminated or solid pieces that replace the stern knee called deadwoods. Sometimes these timbers are located beneath the keel, extending it downwards: this is the case for a number of classic yachts. As the size of the boat increases, these pieces are not made from a single timber. It becomes necessary to join together several pieces of wood along the length of the keel, using plain or stepped scarf joints, and at times the thickness can be doubled by a false keel.

On large vessels, the stem and stern post are also made up of several elements.

The aft section of the boat can be brought up against the stern post to form a 'double ended' hull, but more commonly, the boat has a transverse transom, which will be discussed later on (page 60). When she's given a counter stern it's the centreline structure that is extended beyond the stern post to form the counter extension.

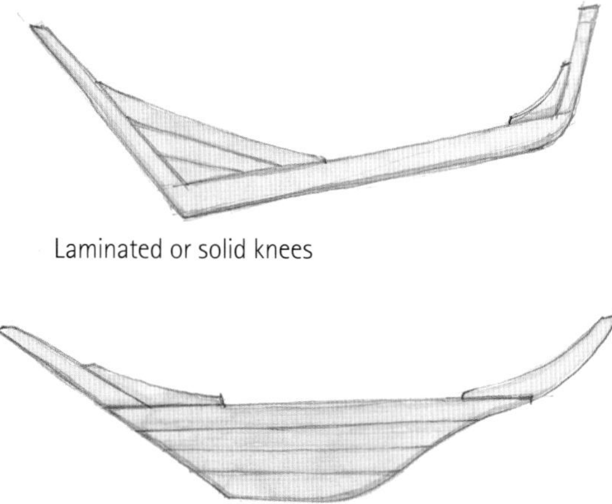

Laminated or solid knees

Hook scarf joint

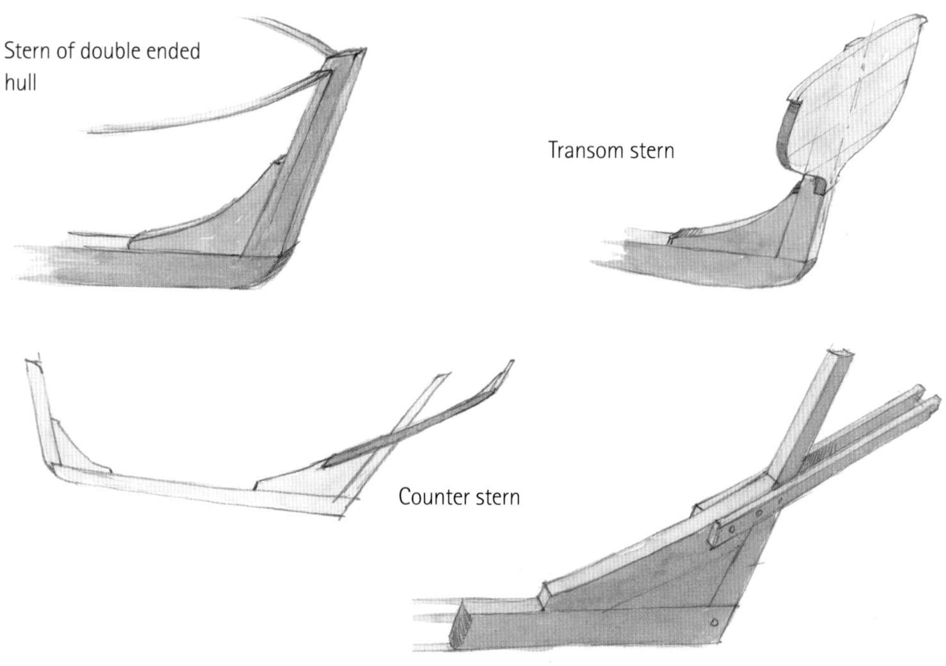

Stern of double ended hull

Transom stern

Counter stern

THE HOLLOW BEAM EFFECT

It is important to know that two parallel timbers, set apart from each other by a series of joining timbers – along the backbone the keel, keelson and floor timbers – form a more rigid structure than would be the case for a beam made from a single timber with the same cross section as the combined parts. This is what we refer to as 'the hollow beam effect', which is used to good effect in other elements of the structure: sheer plank-ribs-inwale or planking-ribs-stringers.

In the same way, but to less effect, a beam with two sections joined to each other, for example a keel and hog, has greater rigidity than a beam made from a single timber with the same cross section.

THE ROUND BILGED DINGHY

The keel of the round bilged dinghy is sawn from a single timber, to the dimensions of the plan, and then carefully braced along its section. This work can be done with the help of machine tools – bandsaw, jigsaw or circular saw, surface-planing machine – as well as from a similar beam section planed down with an electric plane or by hand, until the exact dimensions are obtained.

Backbone with keel and rabbet

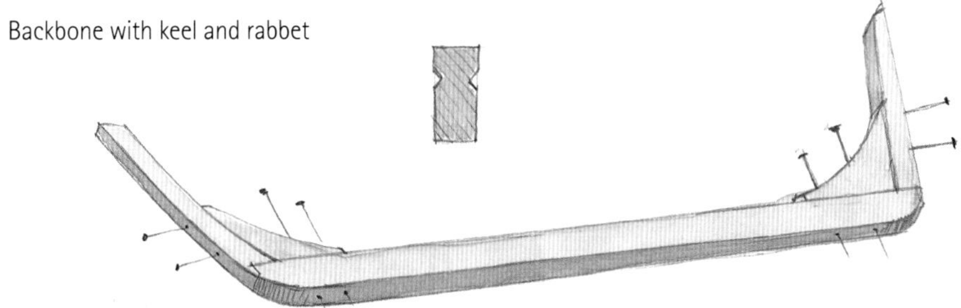

This essential structure is best made from flawless wood, without knots, with a perfectly straight grain, preferably in oak. You will notice in the round bilged dinghy (page 18) that the keel is a straight timber simply joined at the bow and stern post by the stem knee or stern knee, the whole thing being notched with a rabbet. This is the simplest configuration.

For the centreboard version, the top of the keel is shaped to follow the general line of the hull planks and is capped by a hog (this assembly enables a better joint to the garboards – page 14 – than a rabbet, on a boat that has a very wide V-shaped flat bottom).

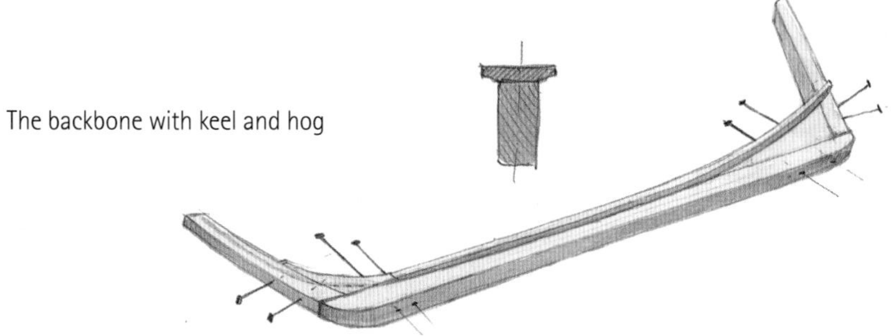

The backbone with keel and hog

The hog extends all the way aft to join with the stern post and lands forward against the stem knee. Above that, you cut out a rabbet on the stem knee and the stem.

The timber for the keel is cut using a framing square (with a 90° angle) and only the exterior angle will be finished later on.

The bow and stern post are usually joined with the keel using mortise and tenon joints before being pegged. This work is done flat, the pieces laid out on the ground or on boards.

The stem and stern knees are selected from curved wood with the help of a template, then cut out with a bandsaw or a jigsaw. These timber pieces are braced and adjusted on the keel, the stem and the stern post, then jointed and pegged with the help of galvanised iron, bronze or stainless steel bolts, after coating adjoining faces with a watertight bituminous or 'blious', a Breton term designating a greasy mix prepared with glazier's putty, red lead, linseed oil, whiting and chopped oakum. Similarly, all the contact surfaces are protected with red lead and then coated in the 'blious' product.

THE BALLAST KEEL

Yachts have largely adopted exterior ballast, either built into the keel or at the end of a fin beneath the hull. This ballast is made from a piece of cast iron or lead, specially made in a foundry and cast in a mould. The ballast is fixed to the keel or the hull with bolts, which also pass through the floors and keelson. However, traditional open craft, small craft with centreboards, dinghies and small working boats, are not generally ballasted; they simply get their stability from the hull shape and from the weight of the crew, who sit on the rail or go out on a trapeze wire if necessary. The heaviest dinghies have internal ballast in the form of small lead or iron pigs secured between the floors. Sometimes, water ballast is also used and the tanks are emptied when the boat is lifted out onto the hard. In any case, the stability calculations will enable us to check that the planned arrangement is satisfactory.

V-BOTTOMED BOAT

The backbone of a V-bottomed boat doesn't differ at all from that of a round bilged dinghy. You are still likely to make the keel, hog, stem and stern post, as well as the stem knee and stern knee, in identical fashion.

THE FLAT BOTTOMED BOAT

The structure of a flat bottomed boat has the particular characteristic of generally lacking a keel (if there is one, it's more reminiscent of a false keel designed to protect the boat's bilges). The flat bottom of the boat is made by joining the planking onto the transverse futtocks or floors.

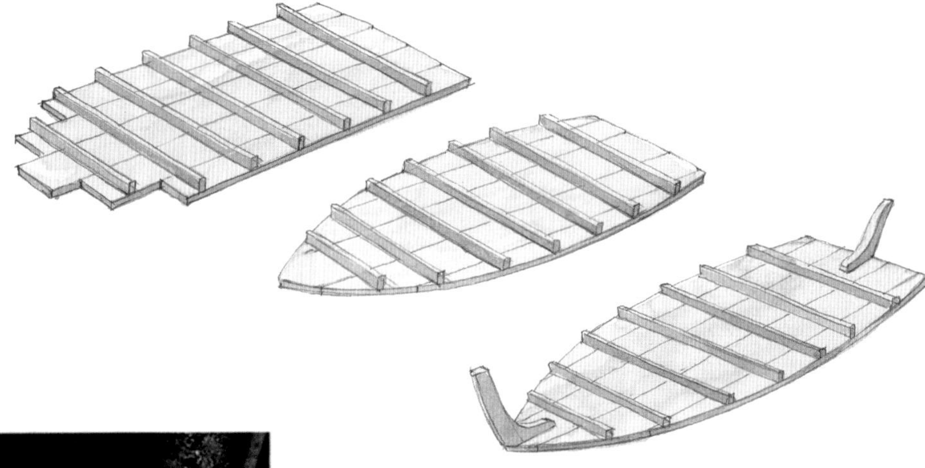

Stem of a flat bottomed boat with its rabbet

The stem and stern post pieces are prepared like a round bilged dinghy, but their assembly doesn't require mortise and tenon joints; the stem knee and stern knee alone ensure the connection with the sole. To enable the craft to be more easily driven through the water, the bottom isn't completely flat: it is slightly raised up forward and aft. This bending (known as rocker) is obtained by heavily loading the bottom, for example with stones, or by 'forcing' it with the help of supports and wedges. Boiling water poured profusely gives the wood flexibility and facilitates the operation.

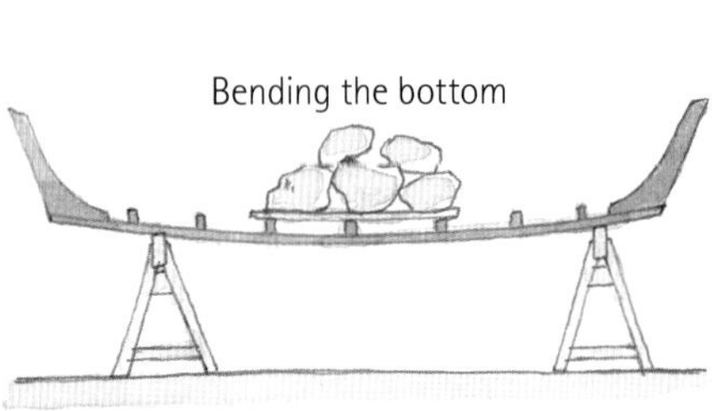

Bending the bottom

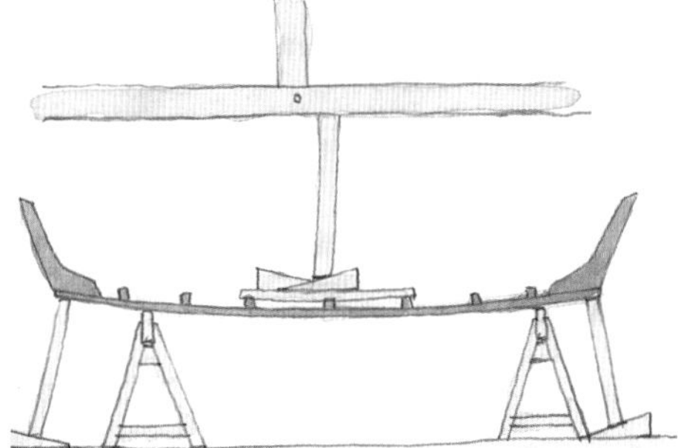

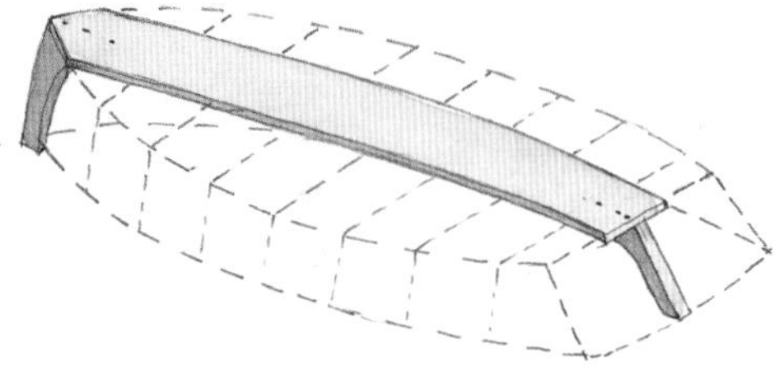

Instead of the ancient method of starting the construction with the bottom, some builders prefer to begin with the frame, which will be laid upside down with the boat upturned (page 63). The stem and stern post are then fitted to the central bottom plank.

RESTORATION OF THE BACKBONE

In terms of restoration, any work on the longitudinal centreline structure generally involves removing either damaged or rotten sections. The repair is made using a scarf joint, which will enable the new timber to be joined securely to the old.

To completely change the stem, the stern post or the keel, is an operation that is a lot trickier, but not impossible. The main difficulty lies in dismantling the old sections by removing the planking, then sawing through the tenon and the joints with the neighbouring frames. During this operation, you have to watch that the hull doesn't distort. Next, the construction begins.

THE FASTENING PROCESS

To fix together the elements that make up the centreline structure, we use blind bolts or metal pegs. The bolts are often made from forged steel and hot-dip galvanised. The head is driven right into the surface of the wood with only a small section containing a thread exposed; just enough to ensure the bolt can be tightened.

In traditional construction, we also use steel pegs, which are simple rods cut to the desired length and driven in like huge nails.

To fix the planking of small dinghies onto sawn frames we use galvanised nails or possibly ones made of ribbed stainless steel; galvanised spikes are used on the largest boats. If the frames are bent, the carvel or clinker planking is then riveted to them. Copper nails are used and they come in various diameters and lengths.

Before putting any fastening in, a hole is drilled for it, the hole having a diameter of less than a third of the diameter of the fastening in small timbers, up to 9/10th the diameter of the fastening in large timbers. The timber and the holes are coated in red lead, white lead, pitch.

THE FRAMES

The backbone of the boat can be compared to our own spinal column with the transverse framing being akin to the ribs of a ribcage.

This structure forms the frame – a set of ribs – which gives the boat her general shape and form. The number of frames is proportional to the size of the boat; they are spaced apart at regular intervals at a distance we call the frame spacing and are individually made up of two symmetrical elements: the frames, joined at the base by a floor timber. Each frame corresponds with a transverse section of the boat, the widest of which is the midship section timber at the fore and aft centre.

Two different types of frame can be used, each with its own qualities. The sawn frame (the shape of which is obtained by contour sawing) is made of oak and the bent rib (also referred to as a steamed rib) is made of acacia, ash or oak.

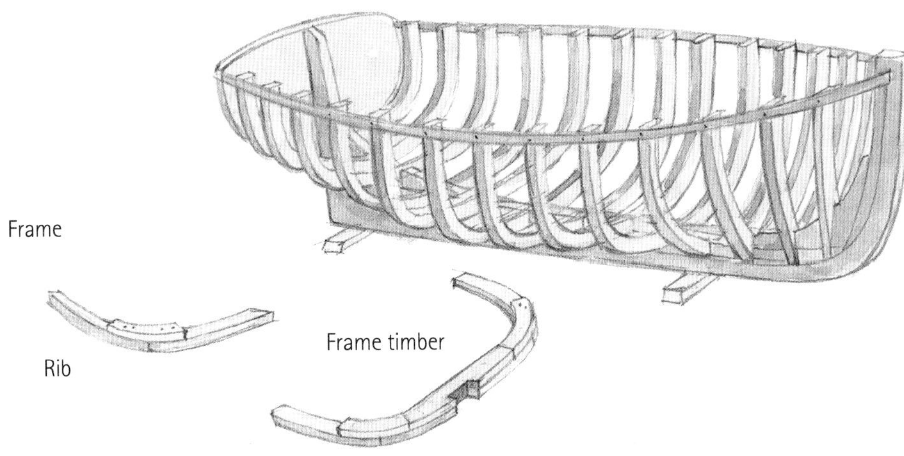

THE SAWN FRAME

Each section of a sawn frame is made by joining timbers together and these determine the transverse shape of a section of the boat.

If the boat is of round bilged construction, as with our example dinghy, some of the components will be curved; they should be cut from curve-grained timber with the help of templates. This requires you to have a large enough selection of curved wood, which is the main difficulty.

Generally, a complete sawn frame is made of two top futtocks, two knees in the middle, two bottom futtocks and a floor piece, which joins the two symmetrical parts (the frames) and fits exactly across the keel.

If she's a hard chine boat, as with our example of the V-bottomed boat, the frame timbers are straight and easier to cut.

A frame with sawn timbers is robust, but relatively heavy. Sawn frames were once used in the majority of boats, from fishing boats through to the largest of yachts.

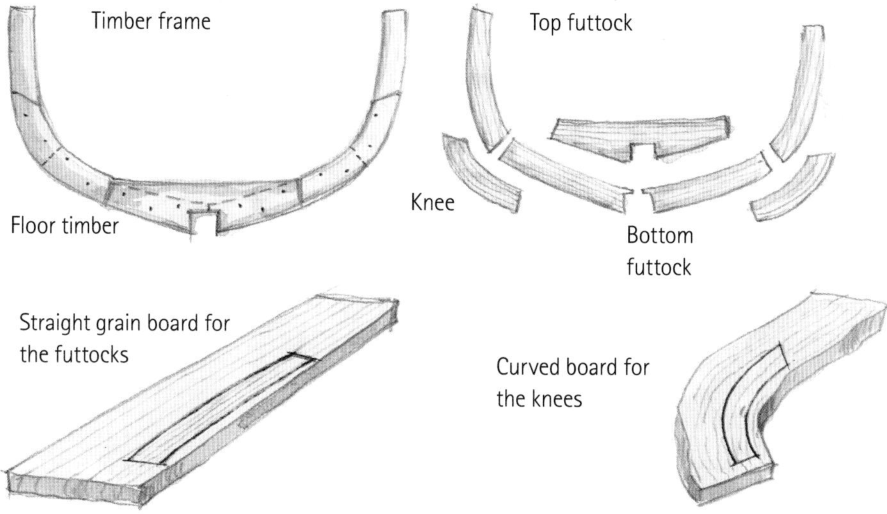

The framework of a round bilged dinghy built with sawn frames, requires prior lofting work, which will be studied in further detail over the page. The amateur will only be able to tackle it after a few attempts, made to get a clear understanding of the process. The sawn frame of a V-bottomed boat is a lot easier to make, while the flat bottomed boat presents little if any difficulties.

In the case of a restoration, each part of a frame timber can be dismantled and replaced, after using a thin bladed saw to cut through all the metal fastenings that link it together, as well as cutting the nails fastening the planking. You should attempt to dismantle the section to be changed without breaking it, so that it can serve as a template.

If you have to change the whole frame, you have to dismantle each element, one by one, and proceed in the same way for the assembly of a new frame. That way you will avoid having to dismantle the inwales and bilge stringers as well as the keelson.

BENT OR STEAMED FRAMES

Initially easier for an amateur to make, a bent frame is made up with straight cut wooden battens, then bent. These fairly slender strips of wood, generally 2 or 3cm wide, are placed in a steam box to give the wood temporary flexibility. The minute it comes out of the steam box, the batten is fitted (bent) to the shape of the frame we wish to make. After cooling, this piece of wood will retain its new shape.

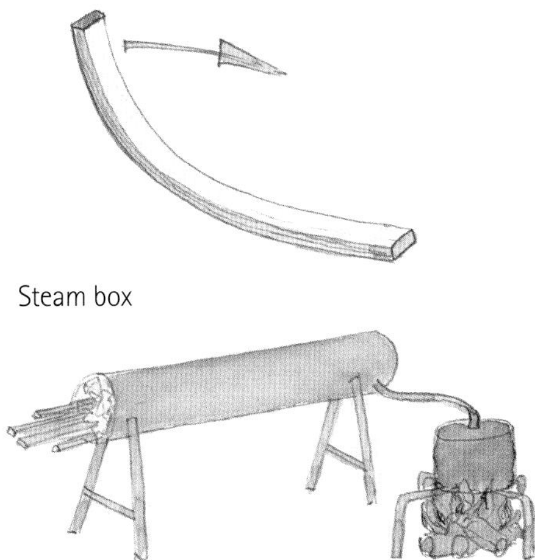

A bent (steamed) rib has the benefit of being able to be cut from straight grained wood, such as acacia or oak, preferably green and easy to find. It also has the advantage of being light and flexible. This type of frame really suits small, light dinghies, yachts or boats that take the ground with each tide.

In the majority of cases, the bent frames are fitted straight to the hull, after part or even all of the planking has been laid. This is the case for all dinghies built on moulds (page 58).

In the case of a restoration, the bent ribs are often found to be broken at the turn of the bilge. In this situation we can 'double' a broken rib (fit a new one alongside the old) as far as the bilge stringer or, better still, partially replace it by scarfing in a new section at the break. If we decide to replace it completely, it may be necessary to remove the gunwale.

TEMPLATE MOULD MAKING

Templates are made from thin wood or plywood and are shaped with the help of nails arranged on the full-scale lofting. These tacks, spaced around 10cm apart, are laid flat with their heads following the lofted curves. To transfer the shape, lie the template material down on the complete set of tacks and press down or even hit the wood with a hammer. The heads of the nails will leave an imprint like a dotted line on the template.

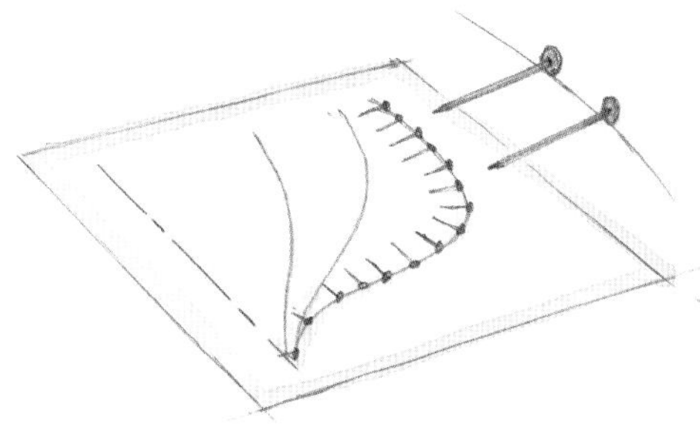

For small craft, we can also use a transparent acetate film on which the shape is drawn with a felt-tip pen and then cut out with scissors.

THE ROUND BILGED DINGHY

For the frame of this dinghy, three methods are on offer: sawn frame, mixed frame or bent frame.

SAWN FRAME

The frame templates or moulds are lofted and cut out from thin plywood, starting from the full scale plan (see page 38 and refer also to page 56). The template will show the various sections of the frame: futtock, knee, floor. Each of them needs to be cut from wood with appropriately curved grain, but the top and bottom futtocks and the floors are easier to find than the knees, which need grain that turns through a much tighter angle. The frames situated in the forward section of the dinghy aren't very curved and are cut from a single section.

All these elements are lofted onto boards and marked with a pencil so as not to mix them up. They are cut with a bandsaw, or possibly with a good jigsaw, taking care to cut them accurately within a cutting margin.

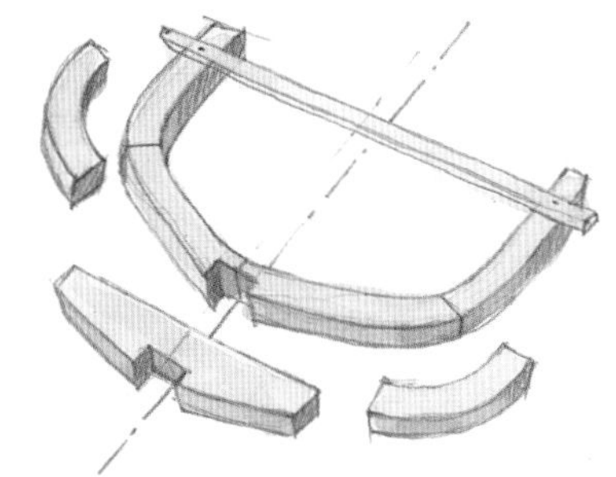

Our example dinghy's framework consists of around 15 frames, or a total of over 100 pieces of wood, which will be assembled on the ground, with the help of pegs or coach screws, then overlaid on the full-scale lofting.

The top futtock heads are held in place by a cross strut, then the frames are erected on the keel in the version without a centreboard (page 18) and on the hog in the centreboard version (page 14). The frames are positioned so that each aft face is situated along the athwartships line of the station in the forward half of the boat and, conversely, so that each forward face is along the station line in the

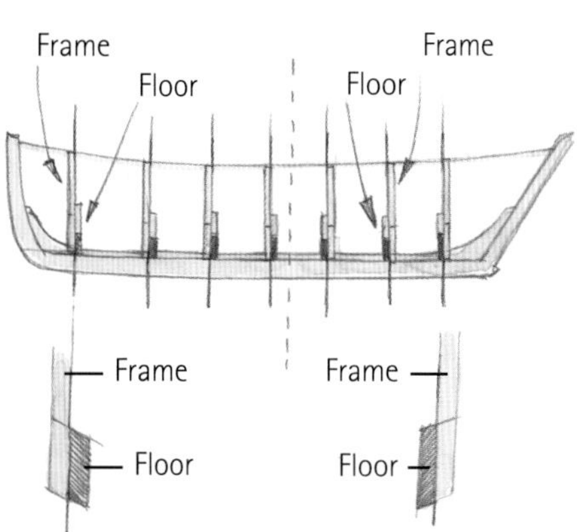

after half (the space between the two frames situated in the middle of the boat is therefore slightly bigger than that between the other frames).

The frames are carefully set up to be perpendicular to the backbone, at right angles to it horizontally and at the correct spacings. Finally the keelson, which doubles the keel above the floors, is positioned flat and is gently fitted onto the floors. The keelson-floor-keel assembly is locked together by metal pegs or bolts, which go right through the keel at each floor.

To support this still unstable frame, provisional shores will be positioned on the ground and in the frame former.

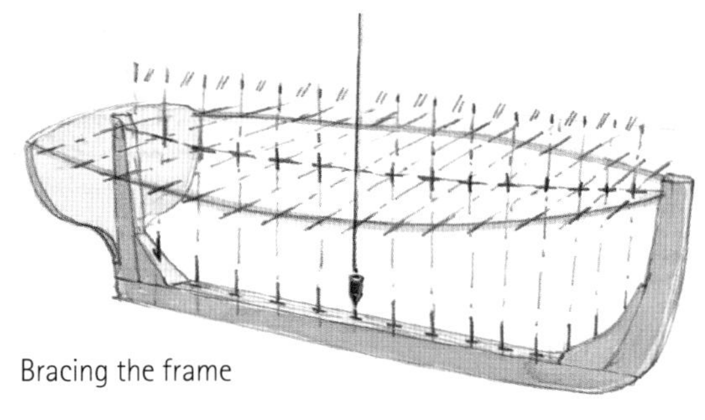

Bracing the frame

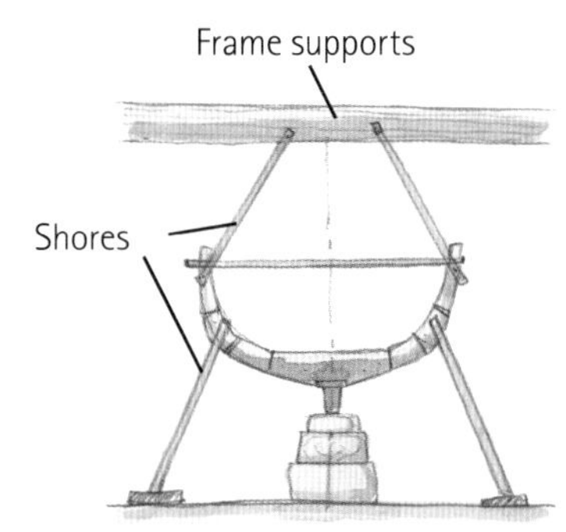

FAIRING THE FRAME

The frames assembled in this way are cut at right angles. By using a long, flexible batten curved over the frames, we can see that it doesn't sit correctly against the midships mould and less so against the other frames. The fit becomes poorer the closer one gets to the ends of the boat where just the edge remains in contact. The fairing operation will consist of cutting the frames with an adze or planing them down, until full surface contact is obtained between frame and batten, to ensure that the actual planking fits as snugly as possible.

This work is carried out along the whole of the outside surface of the frame by moving the flexible batten along the length of each one. This takes into account the changing angle of the fairing (the bevel angle), which alters up and down each frame. The fairing

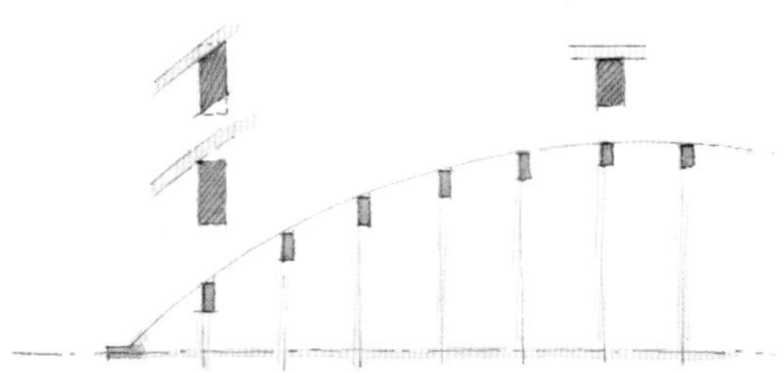

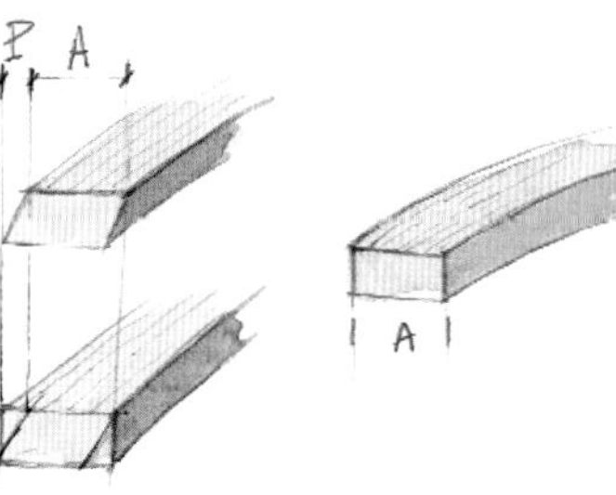

will be considered complete once the batten lies closely against each frame. However, it will be possible to perform a few final touch-ups as each plank is offered up. The bevelling will be repeated in a parallel fashion along the internal face of the frames once the planks are in place. It is worth noting that you can rough-hew each frame before joining it onto the backbone, because you can work more easily at the workbench and only the final touches will be needed on the assembled frame. These old methods have the benefit of only requiring simple tools, such as an adze, or a hand or electric plane.

There is a faster and less laborious method of bevelling, but it requires you to have access to a bandsaw with an adjustable table. Indeed, today, in professional yards, the fairing or bevelling is replaced by the angular sawing of all the timbers, which are directly cut in a thick or thin format – with an obtuse or acute angle – (see yellow box on page 57) thanks to the values given on the lines plan. Such machines are rarely accessible to the amateur builder.

To maintain a constant section along all the frames, and hence uniform contact between frames and planking, it is necessary to plan the amount of wood to be removed during fairing: their dimensions will be increased as a result. If a non-increased frame were to be bevelled, you would end up with one that didn't fit properly against the planking.

Whether you choose the old fashioned way of fairing or bevelling with a bandsaw, you begin by determining the variable angle (bevel) that the side of the frame must have when it is in contact with the planking. For this we use a triangular protractor (a bevel protractor), one side of which is equal to the measurement of the frame spacing (or 25cm in our example) and another that is graduated in degrees.

Working with the adze

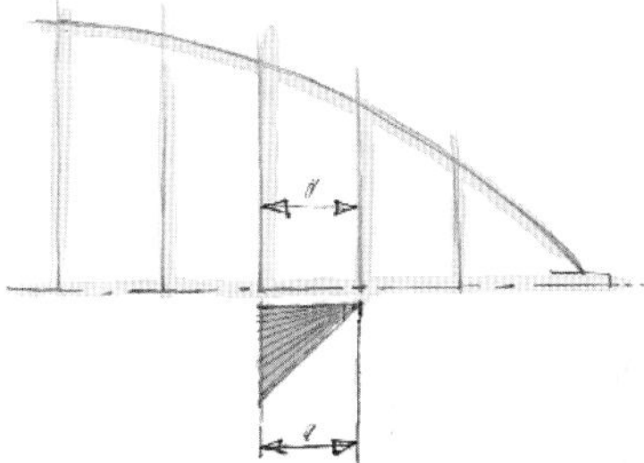

Bevel protractor that is the size of the frame spacing

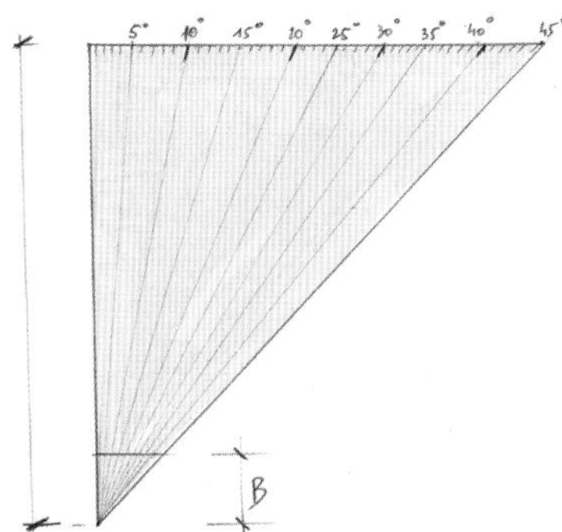

This bevel protractor is made from a small piece of thin plywood. You use it on full scale drawings or the lofted lines of the frames. For example, to find out the angle of rib II at point A, you lie the protractor down on the tangent at A, then read the angle shown where the edge of the protractor meets the adjacent frame III. Still on frame II, to find the angle at point B, you position the protractor on the tangent at B, in the same way as for A, and read off the angle against frame III. You continue in this way along the entire length of frame II at as many points as you like. The operation is the same for all of the boat's frames.

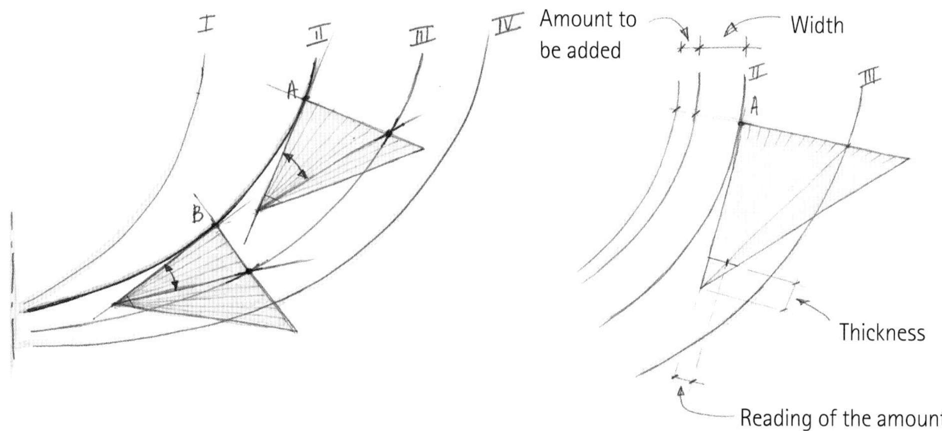

A line on the angle protractor indicates the thickness of the frame. It is easy to read along this line, following the trimming angle or bevel, to find how much to add on to the thickness to determine the line of the inner face of the frame. This variable value is determined for each frame point (A, B etc). You will eventually see that the lines of the exterior and interior faces are not strictly parallel, their distances apart varying along the length of the frame. We will repeat this operation for each of the boat's frames.

It's worth noting here that to be able to cut the frames accurately, the ones sited forward of the midships section must be positioned in front of the rib lines (section stations) on the plan and those sited abaft the midships section must be positioned behind the stations.

The frame templates, which help you to find the right piece of wood from which to cut them, as mentioned on page 53, must take into account the interior contour of the rib not being parallel to the exterior contour.

One last comment about the bevels on the frames: the knees and floors, which lie alongside the top and bottom futtocks, will have their interior and exterior bevels defined by taking this sideways shift into account. In practice, for old fashioned bevelling, you can often make do with identical bevels to those on the futtocks.

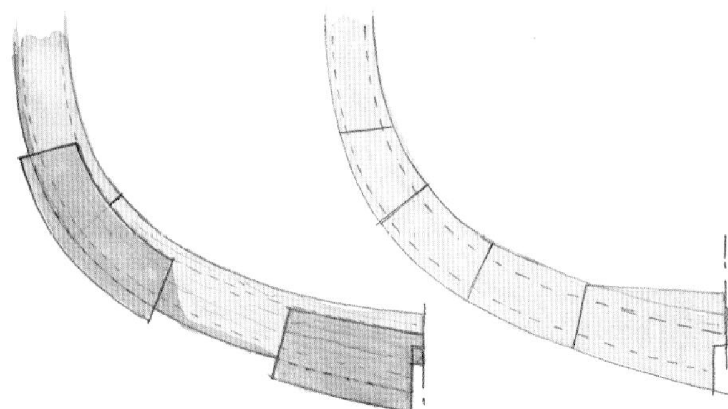

CUTTING SAWN FRAMES USING A BANDSAW WITH AN ADJUSTABLE TABLE

Using a bandsaw with an adjustable table to saw the various parts of the frames – top and bottom futtocks, floors, knees – is done to include the desired bevels, either obtuse or acute. You'll notice that when the futtocks are cut acutely, the knees and floor timbers are obtuse (forming a complementary angle up to 180 degrees), or the other way round, according to the frame assembly types.

The adjustable table on the bandsaw should have a graduated scale of degrees. The bevels required are marked from the moulds directly onto the timbers and we soon see how the bevel varies throughout their length. This makes it necessary for an assistant to gradually change the angle of the table, while the person pushing and guiding the piece of wood tells the other what the desired angles are. You can well imagine that, in order not to force the wood onto the blade, the table's motion must be smooth and the wood passed across it as steadily and as gently as possible. After the planing and marking of all the pieces, frame by frame, to port and to starboard, they are assembled flat, starting with the futtocks and being assisted in their positioning by the template. The knees and floors are then fastened in place.

This technique is a lot more sophisticated than old fashioned bevelling, the mastery of such sawing being the business of professionals or very competent amateurs at least. Beginners should not risk it.

ALIGNED FRAMES

In order to avoid excessive shaping at either end of the hull, especially up forward, some frames can be aligned, that is to say positioned in a perpendicular plane to the planking (and no longer perpendicular to the axis of the boat); these frames will need very little bevelling.

Setting up these two forward ribs at right angles to the planking results in their forming a V shape on the backbone.

MIXED FRAME

In order to limit the quantity of curved wood to be found and to save weight and gain flexibility, you can make the frame of a dinghy by alternating between sawn and bent ribs.

In our study case, seven sawn frames have been planned for; they will be cut up, assembled, mounted and bevelled, then, after fitting the hull planking (see the next chapter), bent ribs will be inserted with two between each sawn frame.

BENT RIB

It's perfectly practical to build a hull entirely on bent ribs, cut along the grain with a portable circular saw. The construction begins on moulds: seven templates are cut from fir, to the shape of frames, and are assembled on the backbone. After that they are bevelled along their edges.

Planks are then temporarily nailed onto these moulds (see the next chapter). Once the planks have been fitted, two bent ribs are inserted between each pair of moulds before the moulds are removed and replaced with further bent ribs.

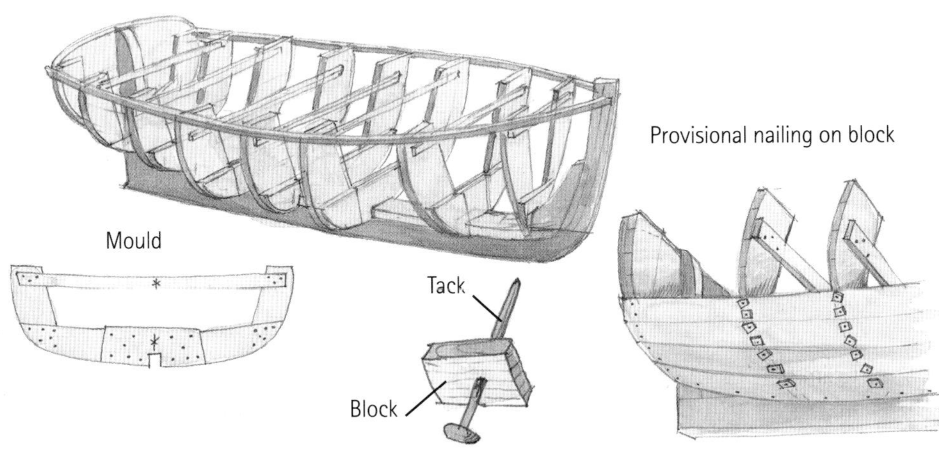

Another method consists of bending the steamed ribs onto a lattice of stringers set into the moulds, which have been reduced by the thickness of the ribs. The planking is then fastened directly onto the ribs. In this case the bent ribs are not fixed directly against the floors; indeed these are less solid than in sawn construction. The floors ensure that the lower planks are fixed at the correct angle to the keel. In the case of a clinker dinghy, you proceed in the same way, but with ever greater ease, the planks being locked rigidly together.

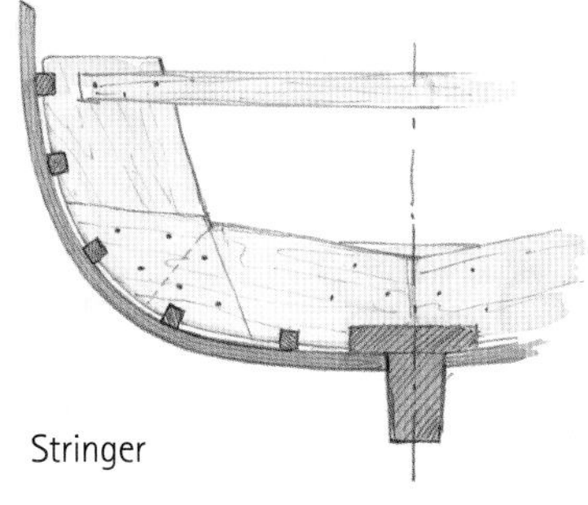

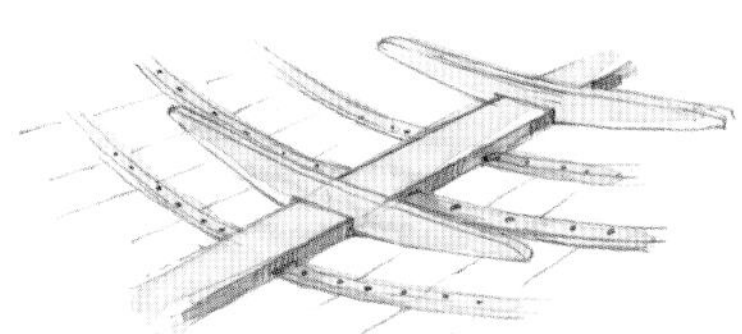

LIMBER HOLES

To finish preparing the frames, you have to cut limber holes in the floors and bottom futtocks on either side of the keel or the hog, to port and starboard. These slots, made before positioning the outer planking, enable the water to drain into the boat's bilges, towards the sump from where it will be pumped.

LAMINATED FRAMES

This more modern technique of glue lamination requires good working and gluing conditions, as well as labour time. It enables curved pieces of all shapes and sizes to be made from straight wood, cut into thin strips. The latter are obtained by stacking them in successive layers and sticking them on a board press, cold bent to give the desired shape. Used for framing, the lamination method has great structural uniformity, because each frame is either made from two sections, port and starboard, joined by a floor timber or from a single moulded timber. This technique also enables curved frames of all sizes to be made and even a complete backbone structure, keel-stem-stern post, all in one. The woods used are often redwoods, which are carefully degreased before sticking them with resorcinol, polyurethane or epoxy glue.

This glue lamination technique, which is inappropriate for traditionally constructed boats, is not out of place on wooden boats of a modern design; it can be used for traditional dinghies constructed using modern processes. For example: laminated frames with hull planking made from sheathed strip-planking or plywood clinker planking (pages 77 and 79).

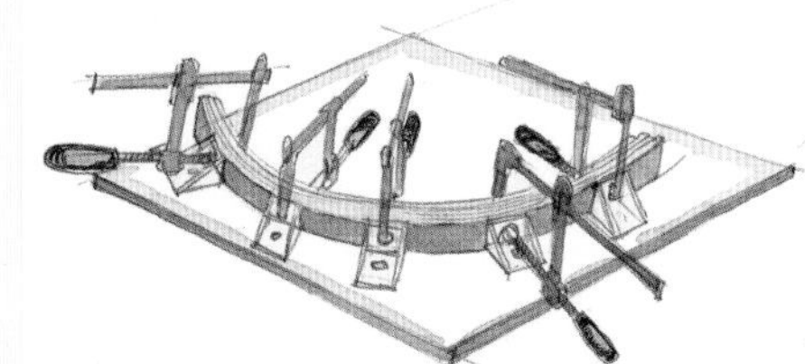

THE TRANSOM

The aft section of transverse framing culminates with the transom. It is worth noting that the rake (angle) of the stern post places the transom in a different plane to that of the frames. As such its representation on the body plan is a distorted view which doesn't represent its actual shape.

Height as seen on the profile drawing.

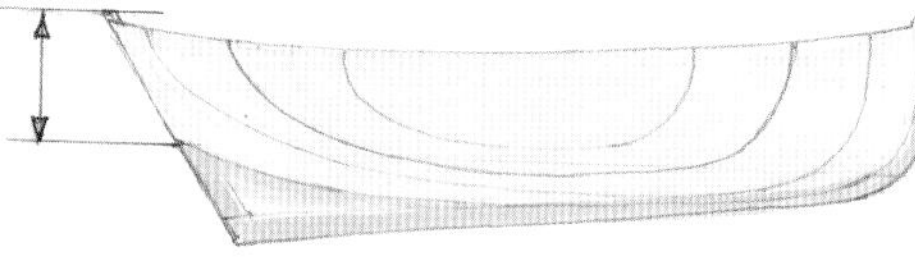

Actual height measured perpendicular to the stern post.

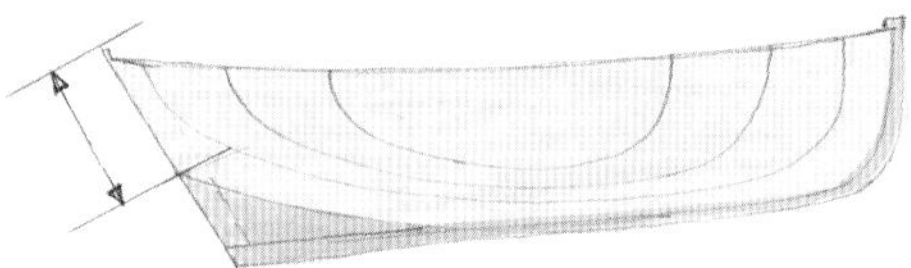

Sometimes, in an extension of the profile plan, there is a drawing showing the actual shape of the transom. If this isn't the case, it is necessary to draw the true shape, by measuring the heights perpendicular to the angled stern post. The bracing of the transom will be lighter or more substantial according to its rake and will be taken into account when cutting timbers.

The planking of the transom is made up from flat boards fastened onto a simple frame called the fashion piece. The timber it's made from is wider than the futtocks of the other frames. They are not linked by knees and floors, but are fastened directly to the planking itself. The whole of the transom is fixed onto the stern post. The fashion pieces and the planking of the transom are trimmed like the frame.

THE RABBET

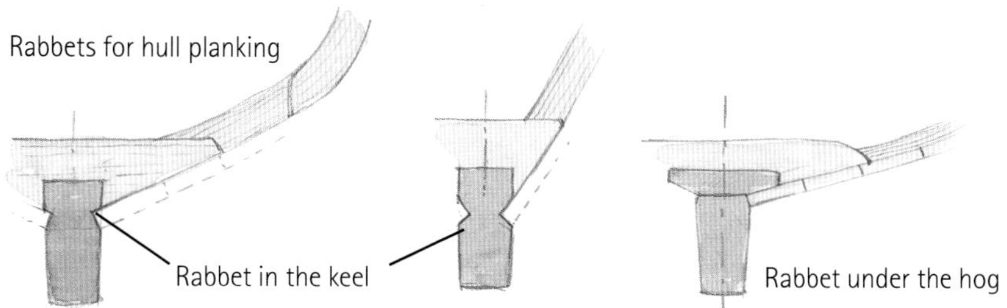

We've just seen the assembly of transverse frames on the backbone of the hull. Before going on to the next stage – the hull planking – you still have to use a chisel or rabbet plane to cut a groove along the entire length of the keel on each side. The groove, referred to as a rabbet, provides the joint between the backbone of the hull and the hull planking. It's a very tricky piece of carpentry, because the angle of the rabbet varies according to how the hull planking butts up to the other timbers. As a precaution, we will make do with roughly hewing it then waiting for the installation of the hull planking before finally shaping it with a plane: the waterlines at the stem and the transverse sections for the keel, indicate the angle of the rabbet.

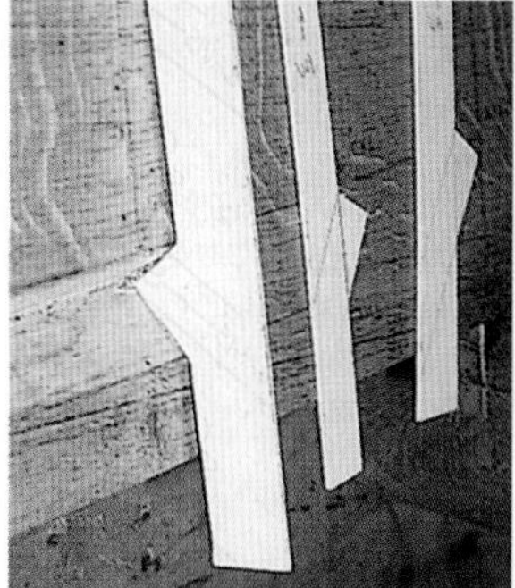
Rabbet templates

STOPWATERS

The rabbet enables a watertight joint to be made between the backbone and the hull planking. Nevertheless, where it meets the various joins in this structure (keel, stem, stern post, stem knee, stern knee...), however good each joint is, water may slowly but surely find its way into the boat's interior. To create a barrier, you lightly drive a peg made from softwood (pine for example) into a hole drilled through each joint from the bottom of the rabbet. As the peg swells up, it will become watertight – hence the name 'stopwater' for these pegs.

You must place as many stopwaters as there are joints along the rabbet. To finish, the ends of the pegs are cut off in a V-shape to match the angle of the rabbet.

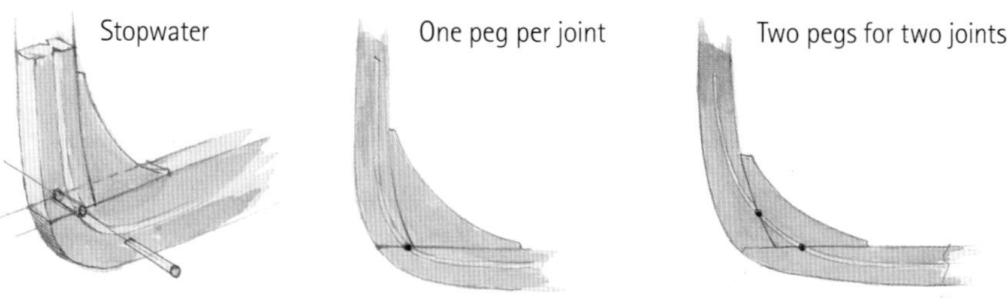

STOPWATERS AND RESTORATION

If the hull planks are removed from the joints along the backbone of the hull, it is possible to check the condition of the stopwaters and to replace them if necessary. However, quite often the hull planking doesn't need changing and the pegs remain inaccessible. In this case you can position a stopwater outside the rabbet, as close as possible to the edge of the hull planking.

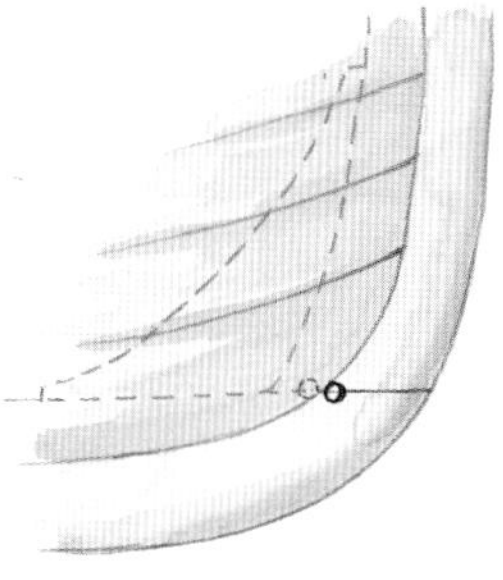

INVERTED OR UPRIGHT CONSTRUCTION

So far construction has been described with the keel down (upright), positioned on blocks, and the frames standing on the keel. This method is generally the only one used for hulls above a certain size. For a small dinghy, however, it is also possible to construct it with the keel in the air (inverted), which helps when fitting the outside planks, but doesn't enable the shape of the boat to be assessed as well during construction.

THE V-SHAPED HARD CHINE HULL

The frame of a V-shaped hard chine hull will be made in the same way as for a round bilged dinghy with sawn frames. Each frame is very simple in terms of cutting and assembly, since the frames are made up of straight elements or have a straight grain. They comprise a top futtock, knee and bottom futtock. If the hull is to be clinker planked, the futtocks will be cut into notchs or steps to receive the planks.

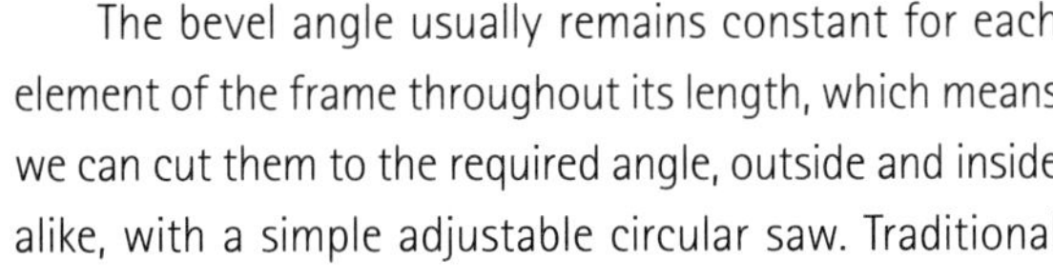

The bevel angle usually remains constant for each element of the frame throughout its length, which means we can cut them to the required angle, outside and inside alike, with a simple adjustable circular saw. Traditional bevelling is unnecessary. The rabbet will be cut carefully, as in the case of a round bilged dinghy (see above).

Hulls with a chine have the distinctive feature of requiring a longitudinal stringer at the corners, embedded in the outside of the frames at the turn of the bilge. In the case of a V-shaped chine hull, this rail fits into the top futtocks and is nailed into the knees from the outside. When the two chines are in position, you can plane them so that the bottom futtocks are flush. The width of the chine provides a good nailing surface for the bottom planking.

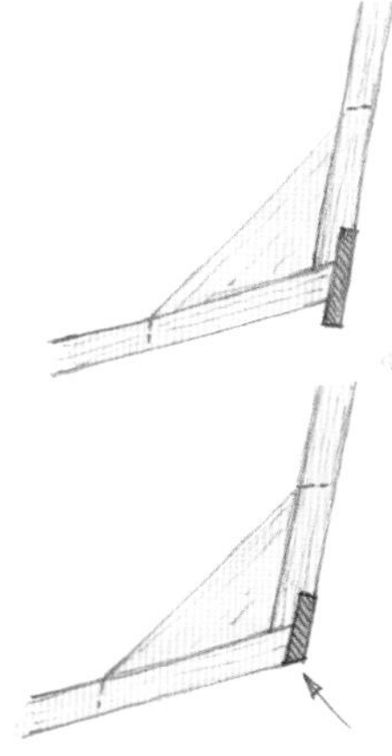

Chine trimmed flush with bottom futtock

THE FLAT BOTTOMED HARD CHINE HULL

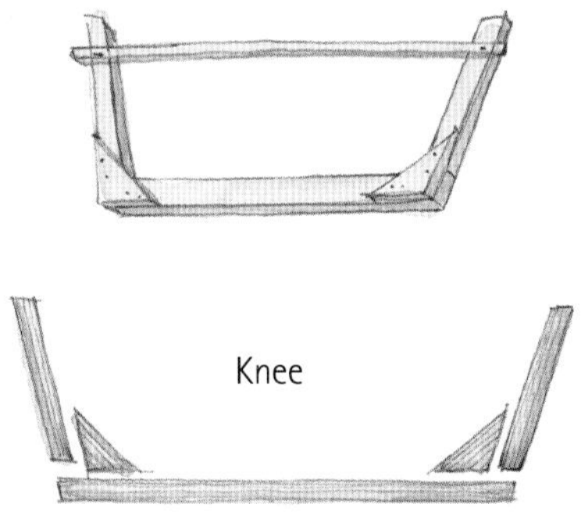

The frame of a flat bottomed boat is the simplest to design. It resembles that of a V-shaped flat bottomed boat, except that the two bottom futtocks and the floor timbers are replaced by a single bottom futtock. You cut each element to the necessary bevel angle with a circular saw. In the case of 'upright' construction on the sole, you add the top futtocks, which are fixed onto the bottom futtocks with triangular knees or scarfs. When using the more common 'inverted' construction, the various frames are assembled separately and then erected on the building frame, ensuring they are carefully set up fore and aft and athwartships. Caution: to be supported by the building frame's horizontal surface, the futtocks should not be cut to follow the deck line (or sheer) but level with the horizontal surface, so they will be cut to the sheerline at the end of construction.

The planking of the central bilge, with the stem and the stern post, is fixed onto the frames, simultaneously ensuring their correct spacing.

If the sides incorporate clinker planking, you cut the top futtocks with notches.

The chines may be laid as they are on a V-shaped hard chine hull, but are flush with the flat bottom (it is a lot more difficult to add these chines on an upright construction).

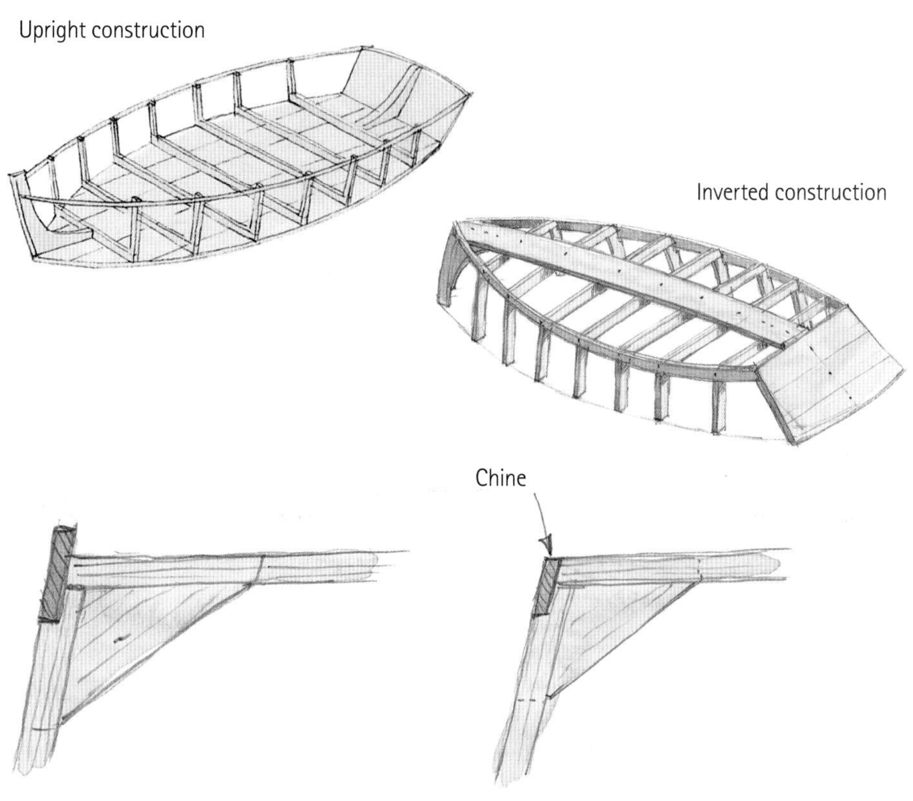

THE PLANKING

To plank means to position the planks forming the boat's hull. For this exterior 'envelope', which we often refer to as outside or hull planking, we use various species of wood: oak, pitch pine, mahogany, khaya and sapele. The two most common methods of planking a hull are: carvel construction and clinker construction.

CARVEL PLANKING

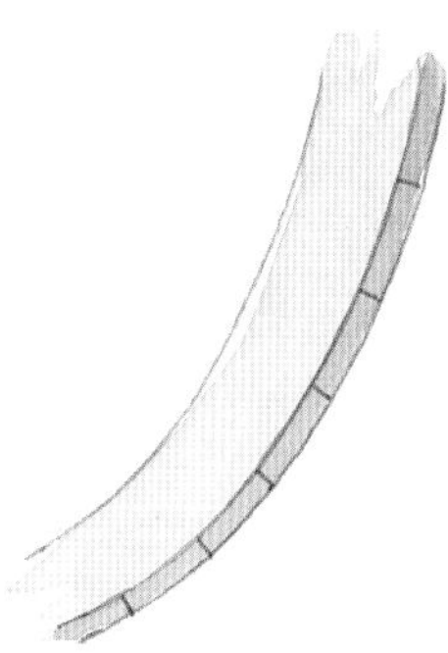

Carvel planking is a construction method consisting of covering the boat's frame with planks placed edge to edge (side by side along their length without overlapping). A run of planks placed end to end and reaching from stem to stern, is a strake. On a small boat, a strake can be formed from a single plank. The planks are nailed or screwed onto the sawn frames or nailed and riveted onto the bent frames. The outside surface of a carvel planked hull is smooth. Its watertightness depends on how well the planks fit together and is obtained using caulking. The hull is caulked by driving a cord of cotton or hemp, sometimes oakum, into the seams between the planks with the help of a tool known as a caulking iron.

It is worth noting in passing that carvel construction (also referred to as a classic construction) requires the construction of a boat according to the shape defined in advance at her design stage: the frame for the hull is built precisely to the plan and the planking is applied to the frame. We'll see that by contrast, clinker construction, at least in its original form, related to a different way of thinking, allowing for more freedom of shaping during building.

CLINKER PLANKING

Clinker construction consists of overlapping the planks – or clinker planking – as you would slates on a roof. They are assembled one on top of the other and held together by means of riveted nails, throughout their entire length, the overlap making them watertight and holding the clinker planks together, without the need for an interior frame, which is only put in place and fixed at a later date. This construction technique enables the future form of the boat to be progressively defined, as the planking is assembled, according to the boatbuilder's taste and experience.

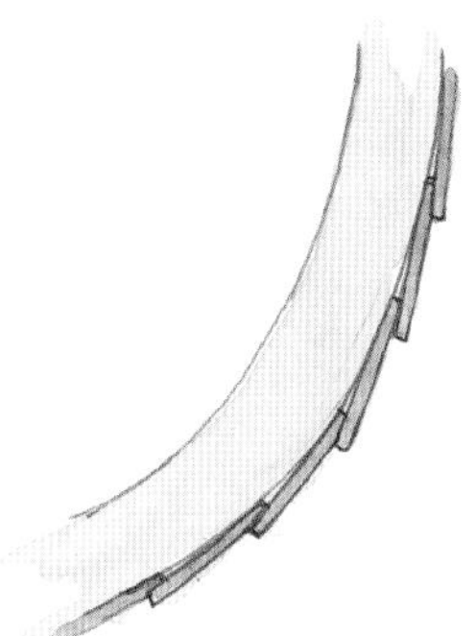

Upright construction or 'keel down'

The interior frame, added at the end of construction, is used to consolidate the whole thing.

This technique, which is still used in Scandinavian countries, is rarely used by amateurs, because it requires great expertise. In the majority of cases, clinker boats are now constructed in the same way as carvel ones, according to a plan drawn up beforehand and lofted to moulds that form a temporary frame, before definitively positioning the frames at the end of construction.

It's this latter method that is described here for the construction of the round bilged dinghy. Those who opt for clinker planking, for which they have a preference over carvel, will do so for aesthetic reasons, for greater flexibility of structure or for lighter weight.

ROUND BILGED DINGHY

To plank a round bilged dinghy, two techniques are used: first, carvel on a sawn, bent or mixed frame, second clinker planking, which only uses bent frames.

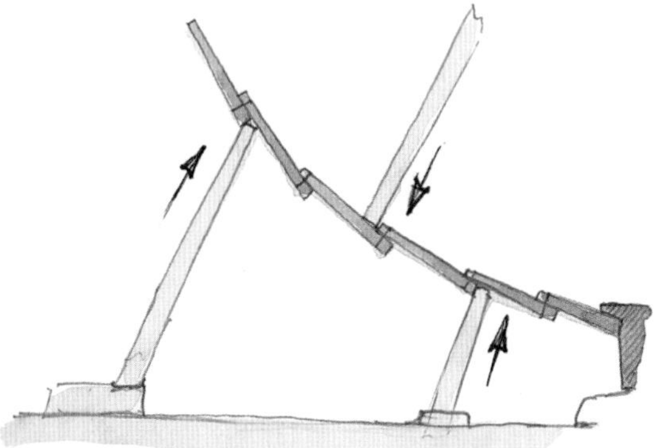
Scandinavian method

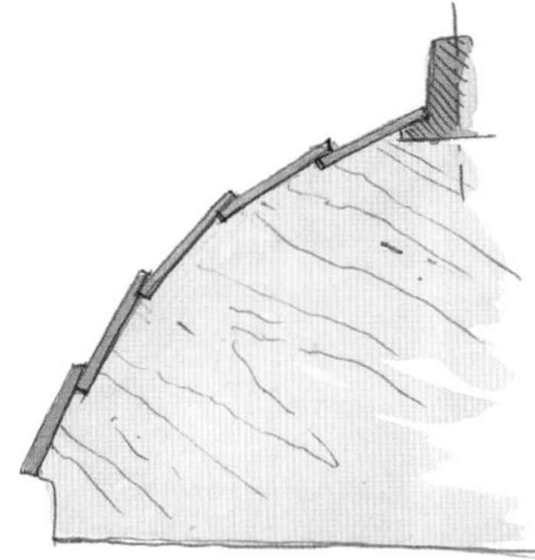
Construction on an inverted keel mould

CARVEL PLANKING ON A SAWN FRAME

To plank a flat surface, like a dinghy's transom, it is sufficient to edge butt the planking, one plank against the next, and nail them to the fashion pieces, the boat's stern frames, which are designed to receive the transom.

To plank the sides of the dinghy, however, and provide a three dimensional curved form, it's not possible to use straight planks. The boatbuilder's true skill is revealed in his or her ability to distribute the different planks across the surface of the hull and define the exact shape of each of them, namely their contour. These operations centre around 'layout' and 'spiling'.

THE LAYOUT OF THE PLANKS

Ten planks from a single piece of timber (long enough to form a full strake from stem to stern of the boat) are planned for each side of the boat so as to cover the whole hull in the centreboard version; you will also need them in the keel version.

You begin by marking out the sheer line points, measured from the plan, which entails marking out the stem, each frame and the fashion pieces: the curved line defined in this way corresponds with the upper edge of the first plank referred to as the sheer strake. It's this curve that defines the boat's sheer and her outline appearance. From the sheer line points, the circumference of each frame as far as the keel is split into 10 equal sections numbered 1 to 10. You proceed in the same way with the fashion piece and the stem.

To arrange the layout of the planks and mark them on the frame, you temporarily nail on slender, square sectioned battens, each of them running through these points: an initial batten for all the sheer line points, a second via points number 2, a third via points number 3, etc. Once this operation is complete, the 10 battens in position represent the seams, lines of contact between the edges of the planks. Each plank is represented by the space left empty between two battens (we only consider the lower sides of the battens, without taking into account their width, as if these battens were simple lines).

In practice, for aesthetic and technical reasons – notably the shape of the planking, the boatbuilder will move these battens slightly, opting instead for curves that are more harmonious to the eye and bend easily, with a uniform separation between them. The closest plank to the keel for example – the garboard strake – gets larger towards the stem and larger still towards the stern post; it fits with its two ends higher than the mark positioned at 1/10th so the plank above needs to be adjusted for 'best fit' with it. Once all the battens run harmoniously, you mark their positions with a line on each frame. The layout is then complete and the shape of each plank can be calculated using the spiling batten.

SPILING CARVEL PLANKS

The spiling operation consists of measuring against the boat's frame, that's to say on the hull, the exact shape of each plank that it will be necessary to cut from a length of straight timber. It's a question of defining the developed shape of the plank, in order that once cut out and bent onto the frame, it takes up the exact space available.

To perform the spiling operation, a new flexible batten – one with a rectangular section and referred to as a spiling batten – is placed between the slender battens representing the contour of the planks (in contrast to the square battens, the rectangular batten can only be bent in one direction). It is offered up to the frame, which will no doubt require it to be drilled, without ever forcing it sideways (if need be, the spiling batten is made from several pieces joined together to run the full length of the hull).

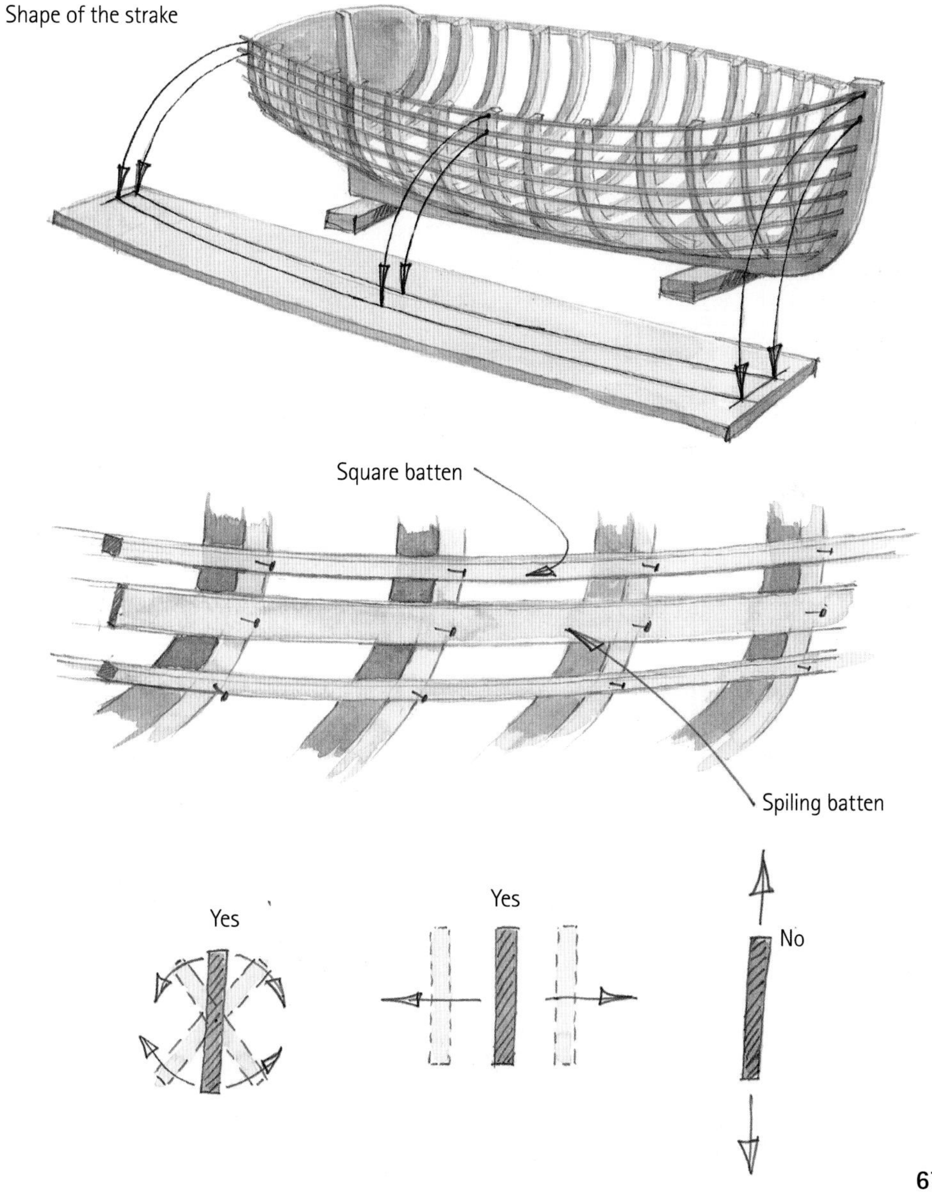

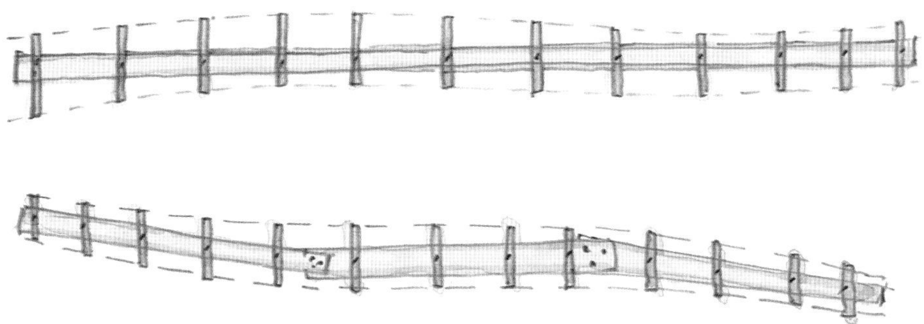

Onto this batten some small wooden pegs or pins (cross battens) mark the exact width between the battens with a square layout: namely the length of the desired planking, which is variable from one frame to another, and from the forward section to the aft section of the boat. If the layout battens obstruct the installation of the pegs, you can take them apart and refer to the mark drawn on the frames. The measurement of the peg (cross batten) is made from the edge of one batten to the same edge of the next batten.

The spiling batten, which then forms a kind of scale, is laid flat on the timber chosen beforehand to be marked onto the required plank.

Determining the shape of a plank with the help of dividers

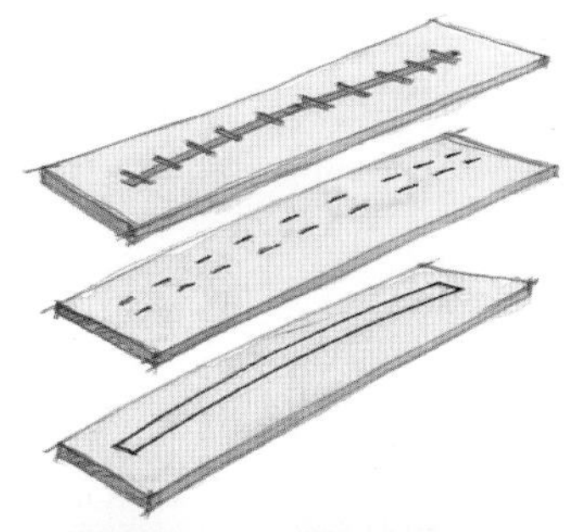

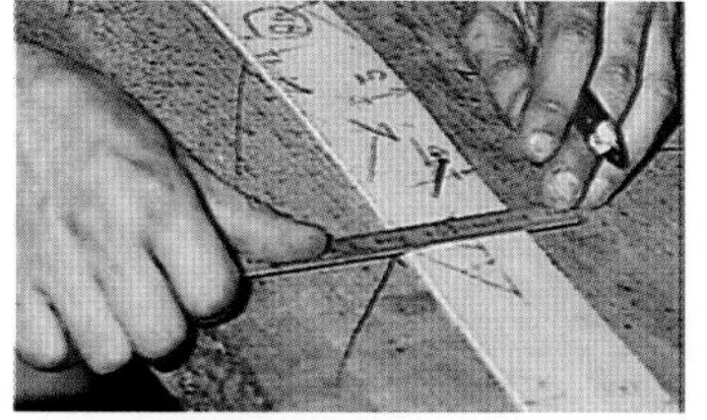

The ends of the pegs or cross battens show the points through which the planking contour line passes. When all's said and done, the spiling batten, complete with its cross battens, is simply a planking template. You use it to choose and mark out the piece of timber that has the most appropriate grain pattern for the required plank. You can, where necessary, replace the pegs with measurements taken from one side to the other of the reference line along the spiling batten or, indeed, transfer the shape to it with dividers, measuring from the edge of the adjacent plank.

Beware: you must complete the spiling of each plank, saw it and install it before moving on to spile the next one. You will find that the same shape is useable for both sides – port and starboard – which are built at the same time.

SAWING

After being drawn out on a dry piece of timber, the plank is sawn (cut out). It is best to use a bandsaw or circular saw but the thickness of the planks on small craft enables them to be cut with a portable jigsaw. Given the lack of precision of these light machines, however, it is a worthwhile precaution to keep a margin of a few millimetres between the line and the cut, and then the plank can be dressed more accurately with a plane.

Unsawn, the plank has perpendicular edges and flat sides. You will have to position it on the frame in its exact position and then shape it. Where the hull is highly rounded, the edges of the planks will be planed down in order to better adjust them to the adjacent planking.

Sometimes you also have to shape it by slightly hollowing out the inner face of the plank to perfectly adapt it to the frame onto which it is nailed. This may especially be necessary at the turn of the bilge (if the hollow is large, you'll have to plan for a thicker plank from the start). In contrast, the 'wine glass' shaped bilge takes a reverse curve close to the keel, needing the plank to be planed to a concave shape. Generally, planks are fitted tight together on the inside edge and opened out into a V along the outside edge for caulking. For this it is advisable to plan, along the entire length of the strake, the space that will enable the caulking oakum to be pushed into it.

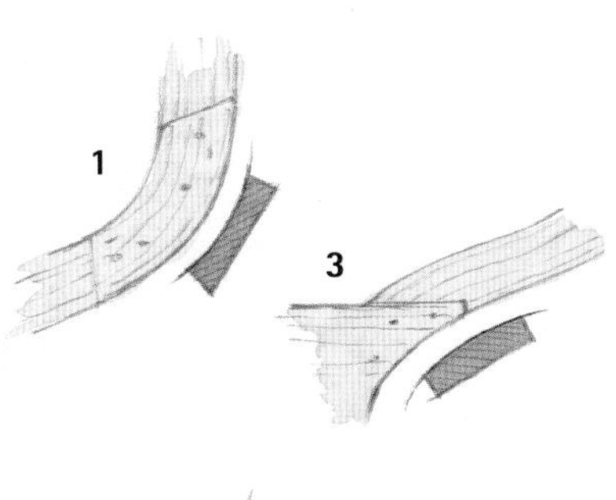

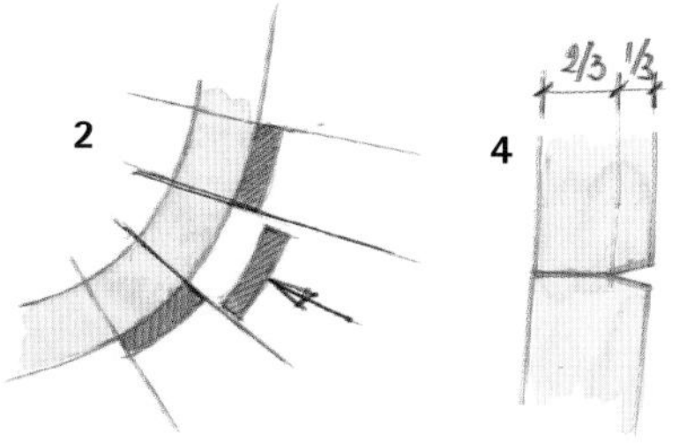

During this adjusting, you will notice that the stiffness of the plank is an obstacle to its fitting closely to the frame along its entire length: when it is fitted up forward, it pulls away aft and vice versa.

To fit a plank perfectly in position, when it is too bent to nail it along its entire length, you first have to make it flexible. This is the purpose of steaming the plank.

STEAMING

Clamping each plank against the next after steaming

After some time in a steam-box, the steaming of the planks makes the wood softer and more pliable (as we previously saw with the bent frames).

The length of time required for steaming depends on the hardness of the wood, its natural flexibility and its dimensions. As regards the planks of a dinghy with a planed thickness of 15mm, just the forward section requires steaming for around an hour. A few trials with a similar size and type of timber will give a better idea of the time required.

Once the plank is out of the steamer, you have a limited time to work with it. Protecting your hands with large leather gloves, you tack the plank against the frame, first by introducing the hood end into the stem rabbet and bending the more curved section at the bows of the boat. This operation is performed with the help of clamps and wedges, the nailing only being started once the plank is fully in place.

THE VARIOUS PLANKS

The process just described, relates to all the hull planks. However, some of them require different treatment.

The boat's upper plank, which follows the sheer line, is called the sheer strake. It's this which encircles the boat and also gives the hull the majority of its stiffness: it is slightly thicker than other planks and we will see further along that it is doubled up, inside the boat, by the inwale, which gives the boat even greater stiffness (it is worth noting in passing that the inwales are drawn and cut out at the same time as the sheer planks).

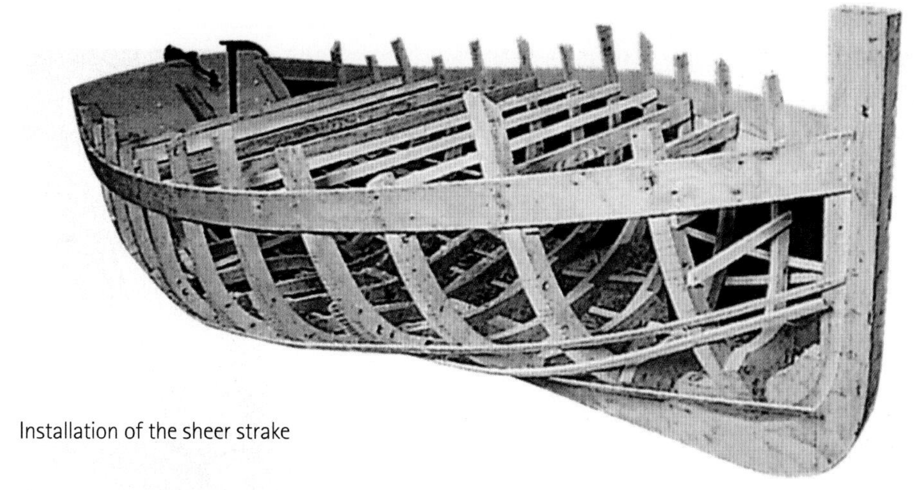
Installation of the sheer strake

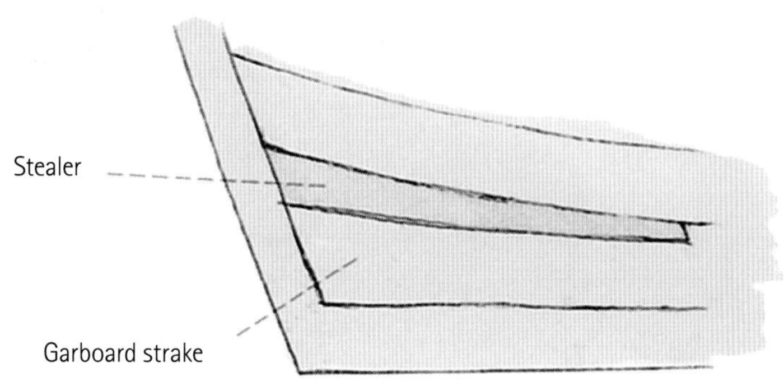

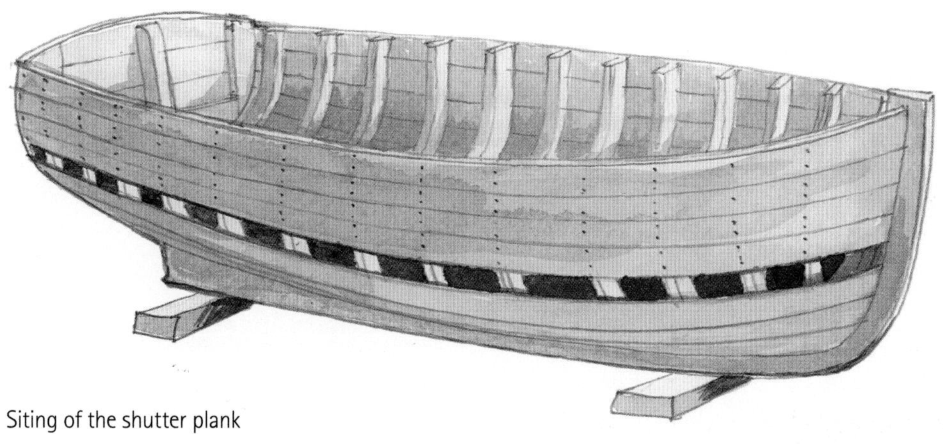
Siting of the shutter plank

In contrast to the sheer strake, the garboard is the lowest plank on the hull, which is directly in contact with the keel, into which it is embedded, thanks to the groove that runs along its entire length: the rabbet. The quality of the fit is particularly important for the future watertightness of the boat.

On a long keeled hull where the shape aft is concave and turns outwards the plank next to the garboard will not lie close to the garboard but tend to rise leaving a gap. This void is filled with a short triangular plank called a stealer (see illustration on previous page).

The planks are progressively added in turn from the sheerline and from the keel. The last free space is thus located at the turn of the bilge, and the plank that will be positioned there – the shutter plank – will need to be fitted with a combination of force and accuracy. It will be imperative to use the exact width of plank, level with each frame, that corresponds with the side in contact with the frame. It is worth recalling that the planks must be very close fitting on the internal hull face.

STAGGERING OF THE PLANK BUTTS ALONG A STRAKE

For the three small boats chosen here as examples, it is possible to make the strakes from a single length of timber, from the stem to the transom, but when the boat is longer, it becomes necessary to make the strakes by joining several planks end to end. The join is made at a frame, the butt joint having to be caulked, and the butts must be 'staggered' from one strake to the next in order to avoid an area of weakness in the planking. You should consider leaving at least a three or four frame separations between the plank butts on two adjacent strakes and at least two if a strake separates them.

Staggering of the plank butts on a clinker built boat

RESTORATION

Here we see the replacement of a damaged shutter plank on an old boat. In all such replacements, the joints in the new plank should be positioned at sawn frames, to which it will be fastened. If it's a question of bent ribs, the joints will be made in the spaces between frames with a nailed and riveted 'butt strap' spanning the joint.

On an old boat, changing the garboard strake or repairing the rabbet, often eliminates annoying leaks, while the replacement of the sheer strake helps to provide renewed stiffness in the hull.

CARVEL PLANKING WITH MIXED FRAMES

The description given for carvel planking on sawn frames remains valid for mixed frames. It is worth remembering that in this case, only seven sawn frames are in position at the start of the operation. As a result it's on them that the planks are supported, their spiling carried out, their positioning determined and their nailing done.

Once the hull is planked, you can add the bent ribs, which are bent directly inside the hull after they've been steamed. To make this work easier, the bent ribs will be positioned prior to fitting the shutter plank, which enables the use of clamps to hold them against the hull more effectively. For the same reason you will always be able to retain a space for one or two more clamps in the topsides of the boat or in the bilges. Immediately they are in position, the bent frames are nailed from the outside, into the pre-drilled holes in the planking.

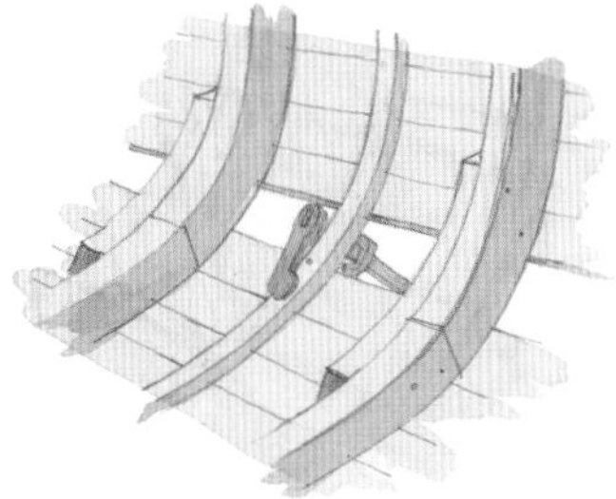

CARVEL PLANKING WITH STEAM BENT FRAMES

In this case, the planks are spiled and positioned on seven temporary moulds (page 58), to which they are nailed or screwed temporarily. The hull is open planked, which involves positioning every other or every third plank. That done, the frames are bent and fastened as described for the mixed frames. It is then possible to complete the planking, by positioning the missing planks. Finally, the moulds are dismantled and replaced by the bent ribs.

CLINKER PLANKING WITH STEAM BENT FRAMES

The operation for distributing the clinker planks is performed in the same way as carvel planking with the exception that each piece of clinker planking is overlaid onto the previous one, which requires a larger plank width. For the spiling of each clinker plank, you place the pegs representing the width of the clinker plank, one side overlapping the previous clinker plank, the other being supported on the mould. Next all the pegs are brought together by a spiling batten positioned on their outside face.

The overlap value in our example measures 15mm. The planking must be done by starting with the garboard and finishing with the sheer plank. For this you use specially made clamps, called wedging clamps or nippers, that temporarily hold the clinker planks together while they're being fastened.

When positioning the clinker planks, care must be taken over the adjustment of their overlaps, on which the boat's watertightness depends.

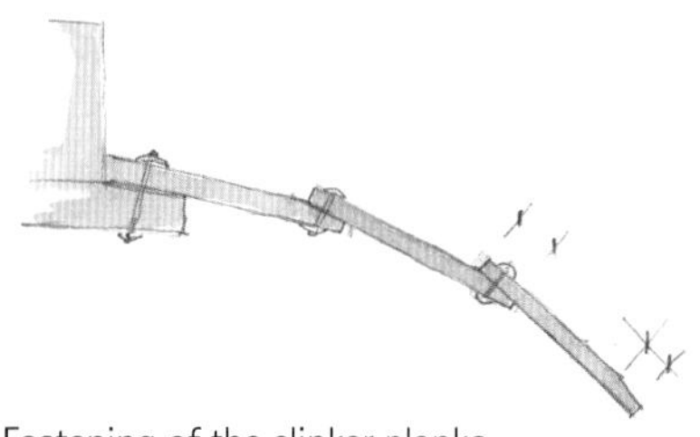

Fastening of the clinker planks

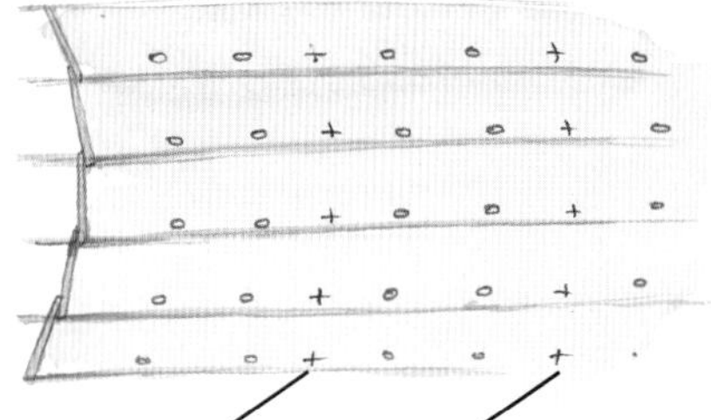

Space for the nailing of a frame

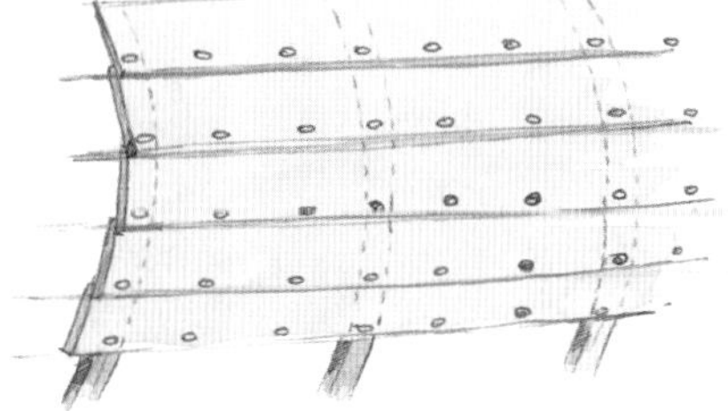

The nails are set out along the planks to leave enough space for fastening the bent frames that will go in later. As each plank lands on the stem rabbet, they stop overlapping each other and are close-fitted side by side; this requires a tapered rebate of around 20cm in length; the same thing happens at the transom.

The fastening of the planks with copper nails isn't a particularly tricky operation. Nevertheless, as the quality of the clinker boat depends on it, it will be necessary to put in a little practice beforehand on a few offcuts of wood. You drill the two clinker planks to be joined together and you hammer in the nail. The roove is put on from the inside and the tip of the nail is cut off around 2mm from the roove. The surplus is then hammered over and spread against the roove, while an assistant holds the head of the nail from the outside with a heavy hammer.

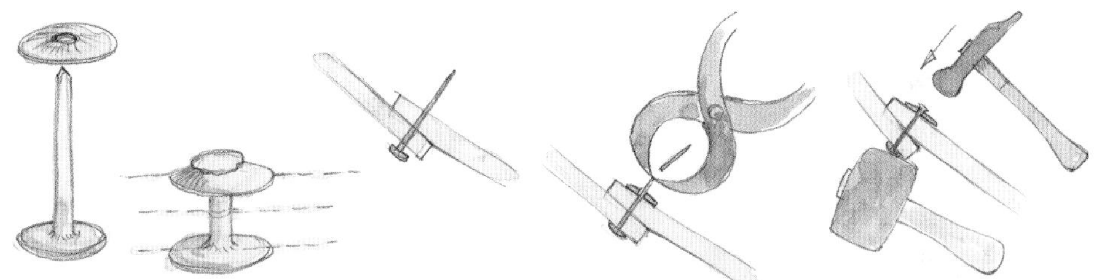

Once all the clinker planks are assembled, nailed and riveted, the bent frame can be added, as per the carvel planked hull with mixed frames.

V-BOTTOMED HARD CHINE BOAT

In the carvel or clinker construction of a V-bottomed hard chine boat, layout and spiling are simplified. Indeed, you often make do with practically straight planks for the sides if the V forms a constant angle along all the frames. Nevertheless, it is advisable to adjust the edge of the garboard, in contact with the keel, within the rabbet. The bottom plank furthest outboard from the keel takes on a semicircular shape as its edge follows the chine.

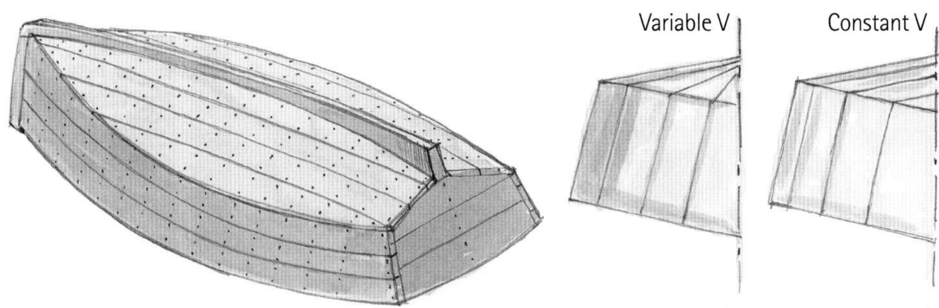

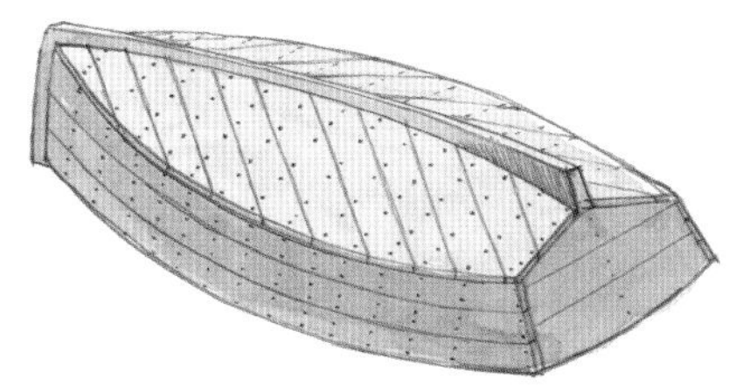
Diagonal bottom planking

If the angle of the V, which is known as the deadrise, varies, it will be necessary to spile the planks. In either case the bottom is made up of carvel planking, even if the sides are clinker. You can also set the bottom planking diagonally, which requires shorter plank lengths that don't need spiling, whatever the change in the angle of the V.

CONSTRUCTING THE FLAT BOTTOMED BOAT

In the case of upright construction, the bottom planks are already in position. If it is inverted, they are added to either side of the central plank, then cut and planed along their edges to make them flush with the chine rail. The layout of the side planks, with carvel or clinker construction, is simple: indeed all the planks have a constant width and their sides are straight, except in the aft section of the lowest plank, which is planed up to the waterline. The general sheer of the flat bottomed boat is created by pushing the sides of the hull out round the chines from transom to stem. The carvel planks must be carefully fitted edge to edge with a caulking groove to ensure a watertight hull.

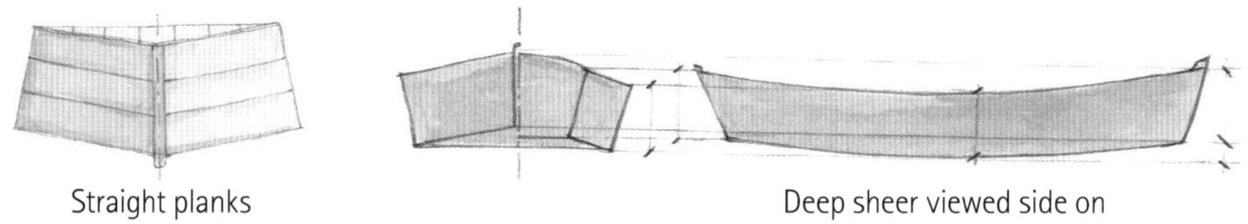
Straight planks

Deep sheer viewed side on

CAULKING

The caulking of small craft with carefully constructed carvel planks is done with a cord of cotton or hemp of small diameter. The sides of the planks are covered with a coat of primer, which most often comprises a red lead substitute*. The caulking cotton is pushed into the V-shaped opening of the seam using a caulking iron and mallet. It has to be done gently, without forcing it, taking care to fill along the entire length of the plank. If the strake is in several parts, the joins will also be caulked.

Another coat of protective paint is applied along the seams, followed by a filler designed to finish the job off tidily. For this you use a glazier's putty, rich in linseed oil, to which is added red lead powder or a modern substitute.

On a boat constructed in a more traditional manner, or for the restoration of an old boat, the seams between the planks may be too wide to be caulked with stranded cotton. In this case you use oakum or tarred tow, rolled over itself, which has a greater volume and will be able to fill the larger gap.

* Use of red lead is forbidden today: it has been replaced by a non toxic orange protective paint to counteract corrosion which makes the wood rot resistant.

MODERN PLANKING TECHNIQUES

For some years now, in addition to the traditional planking methods, boatbuilders have been using alternative 'modern' techniques: glued unsheathed strip-planking, moulded wood or plywood, which are generally simpler to carry out and, at times, offer a weight and time saving – and they result in a more easily achieved and doubtless more permanently watertight hull. For some sailors these techniques evoke yachting of the 1950s, which has rightly led to boats of this age forming part of the 'classic yachting' scene. More recently these modern techniques have been used by designers and builders for all sorts of craft: small work boats, day boats and 'classic' cruisers. This section of the book covers the particular features of these methods, which form part and parcel of the continuing evolution of traditional construction.

STRIP-PLANKING

These two processes – unsheathed and sheathed strip-planking – are used for a round bilged carvel type hull, often assembled on a former, whose bent frames will be positioned at a later date. You can also use the unsheathed strip-planking construction method on a glued and laminated framework.

Planks that would need to be spiled for carvel construction are replaced here by 'strips' of wood that are roughly square in section and considerable narrower than either carvel or clinker planks. The upper and lower edges of these strips are hollowed or domed, so that when they lie together there is an increased gluing contact surface. Once bent into place, the strips are both edge glued and edge nailed to each other. For this you use polyurethane or epoxy glues, which ensure adhesion and good watertight joints, as well as hot dipped galvanised nails or gripfast nails.

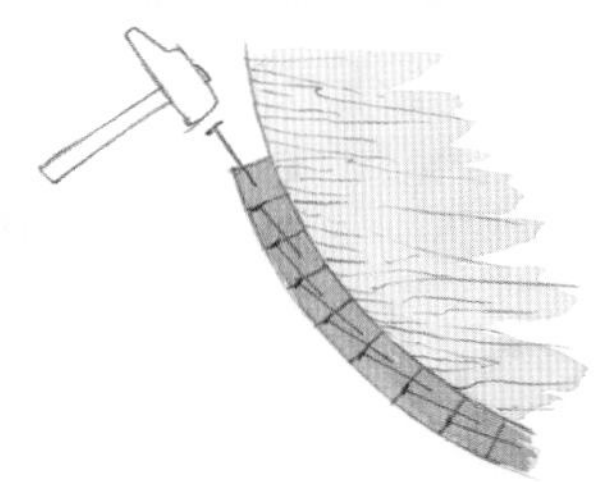

To improve the build integrity, the strip planks are moulded to have convex and concave sides that match with the next strip above or below. This enables perfect adhesion between the strips without having to get them to fit, whatever the shape of the hull. With the appearance of epoxy resins an even simpler method is used today. In this case you don't modify the side of the strips. Instead, once you have completed the assembly of the planking, the spaces that appear between the strips are filled by coating the whole lot in thickened epoxy resin. After drying and sanding, a layer of fine glass cloth material will be laid right across the surface of the epoxy saturated planking. On becoming transparent, the glass material lets the wood appear, and if the solid wood strips are selected for the fineness of the texture, the colour and the grain, the result could well be flattering and deserving of a varnished finish.

The technique is simple and fast if you don't take into account the fitting of the strips, but the sanding phases are numerous and tedious.

In the case of contemporary strip-planking, which has certain similarities to that which has just been described, lamination plays a dominant role. Several layers of glass material are laminated onto both the internal and external surfaces of the planks. These layers are carefully saturated in epoxy resin with any air being removed, and built up until the necessary lamination thickness is obtained to ensure sufficient strength in the hull. The wooden strips, selected from a light species of wood, only serve as a former, because the wood disappears under the outer laminations. This process, which produces hulls with great strength, can also be used to build large boats. The numerous hours of work devoted to exterior and interior lamination, to the handling of materials and resins, to sanding and coating, are a far cry from working with wood.

COLD MOULDED CONSTRUCTION

With this construction method each plank is made up of several layers of thin strips of veneer (measuring 1.5 to 3mm in thickness), most of which are assembled on the framework, which is temporarily made up of transverse moulds and a fairly tight network of battens. The various layers cross over each other, at alternating 90 or 45 degree angles. The quality of the adhesion through fastening and gluing of the layers, will depend on the consistency of the planking. When well made, it will be both light and particularly stiff. To achieve this you need to take a great deal of care and spend a huge amount of time on it. Hulls constructed entirely from cold moulded wood are, today, largely reserved for prototypes.

Another use of this technique consists of sticking together one or two layers of veneers of moulded wood, over the top of a hull made of strip-planking, to strengthen the whole thing and make it impossible for the strip-planks to come unstuck from each other, whilst ensuring additional watertightness.

PLYWOOD PLANKING

In contrast to the modern techniques mentioned previously, plywood planks need to be spiled. The same techniques and traditional construction methods are used with the only difference being the substitution of sheets of marine quality plywood for solid timber.

Plywood seems to have been invented specially to enable easy and quick construction of so-called 'chine' boats or more correctly boats with 'non compound curves', such as the two boats used as examples in this book, as well as the dory type, sharpie and a number of light dinghies, one design keelboats and small cruisers. For boats with non compound curves, plywood can be used, provided that the hull shapes have been designed to produce developable planks (cylindrical or conical development). The bending of the plank over the actual frame of the boat or over a mould with sacrificial moulds, is carried out without steaming and almost effortlessly.

On round bilged boats built of plywood, the clinker technique is often favoured. The spiling of clinker planks is done in the traditional manner on the frame. Old boat designs with wide clinker planks took into account the development of each plank; such a design could thus be used in plywood construction without it being necessary to make modifications. Though the flexibility of the material makes the bending process easier, spiling should still be as accurate as possible. In the contemporary design of small working boats built of plywood, the technique of the wide clinker plank is the most frequently used.

Construction with narrow clinker planks – such as the two round bilged dinghies used as examples in this book – allows all kinds of hull forms and gives the designer freedom and ease in the development of the plans. This ease is something that will be transferred to the builder when planking the hull: the bending and, above all, the twisting process is easier with the narrower planks, though the number of clinker planks increases the build time somewhat.

We understand that the distribution of the clinker planks – wide or narrow – and the quality of their shaping is as much technical as aesthetic. The presence of the bevel edge formed by the overlaying of the clinker planks, in addition to the considerable contribution to structural strength, will clearly highlight their curves and give the shape good rigidity throughout. Plywood clinker planks can be nailed or screwed to each other. They also have to be glued down so the hull is perfectly watertight. For this, thickened epoxy resin is most commonly used.

If you plan to build a round bilged hull with carvel rather than clinker planking, you can use plywood in a mixed technique: with ply planks for the bottom and topsides, on either side of a rounded bilge made from unsheathed strip-planks or shaped wood. Furthermore, there is nothing to prevent you from spiling the plywood planks, in exactly the same way as solid wood and attaching them with halving joints as you would with a canoe or on internal half-lap jointed chines.

Plywood also enables you to use the cold moulded technique, which can incorporate several criss-crossed layers of plywood planks.

THE STRINGERS, JOINING PIECES AND FRAME REINFORCEMENTS

To reinforce the boat's frame you add various joining and strengthening pieces to the inside of the hull. Together with the frame and planking they form a rigid assembly that cannot be bent out of shape. The main joining pieces are the longitudinal keelson and stringers. In the horizontal or athwartships plane, knees are added wherever it proves useful.

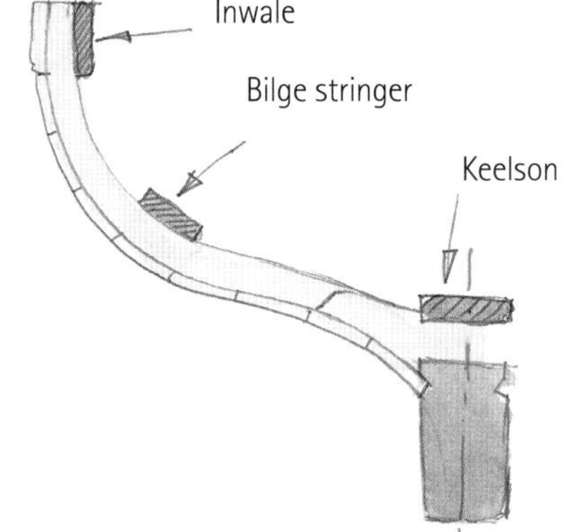

On large vessels, the increased number of joining pieces is directly linked to the complexity of the framework. Clamps and inboard planks take up the whole frame throughout its entire height. Each piece is doubled or even tripled. The inwale, for example, receives a counter-beam and sub-beam; the tweendecks are supported by big knees; imposing breasthooks, grooves and beams stiffen the horizontal plane and the uprights contribute to vertical stiffness.

If you consider that the frame of a square rigger could comprise hundreds of assembled parts, which complemented and reinforced each other, you can but marvel at the skill of the old boatbuilders.

These joining or reinforcing pieces are made from the same species of wood as the rest of the frame. Oak is widely used for classic yachts, but so too are red woods, while locally sourced wood is used for small dinghies.

In the case of the restoration of an old boat, these timbers are of particular importance, because they are quite easy to fit from inside the boat. You will give renewed stiffness to a tired boat by adding a sub-beam or a counter beam, by putting in a new bilge stringer, or even a keelson, a timber often missing from small dinghies originally.

THE ROUND BILGED DINGHY

The longitudinal joining timbers of the round bilged dinghy reinforce the frame along three main lines: the keelson or the hog, already in position horizontally above the keel; the bilge stringer which bends at the turn of the bilge and the inwale, placed vertically, level with the line of the sheer plank (see 'hollow beam effect', page 46).

THE KEELSON

It is worth remembering that by lying flat on the floors, the keelson can be set into them. The whole thing is interlocked by bolts that go through the keel, the keelson and the floor.

The keelson, cut lengthwise from wood with a straight grain, runs from forward to aft where it comes up against the stem and stern knees.

THE INWALES, RISERS AND BILGE STRINGERS

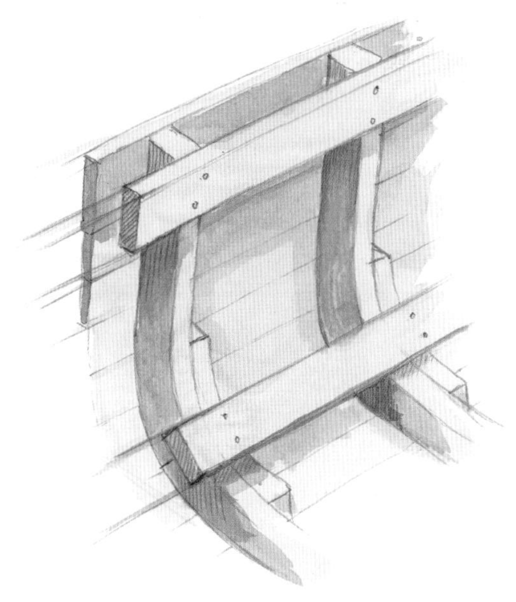

The inwale doubles the sheer plank on the inside face of the frame and forms an especially strong ring on either side of the hull. Its position and fit is practically identical to that of the sheer plank.

The positioning of this timber requires one hour's steaming for the bending of the forward section. Its ends butt up against the stem up forward and against the fashion pieces aft. The creation of a template of the right length will make positioning this sizeable timber easier. The inwale is nailed onto the sawn frames and you can also nail or bolt the sheer plank-frame-inwale assembly. In the case of bent (steamed) frames, the inwale is always nailed and riveted.

In an open dinghy (one that doesn't have a deck), the inwale is often replaced or doubled up by a riser positioned around 15cm below the heads of the frames.

The bilge stringer, positioned right the way round the framework at the junction between the futtock pieces and their knees, reinforces this assembly from frame to frame. It may be stopped on the final frame up forward and in the aft section in front of the fashion piece. This bilge stringer is spiled in the same way as a plank, nailed onto the sawn frames and nailed and riveted onto the bent ribs (clinker or carvel).

THE OPEN DINGHY GUNWALE

In an open dinghy, the frame heads are often covered by a gunwale capping, cut to shape and added to the structure. You cut them from wood with a curved grain, with several pieces joined together, or with a square section timber that is bent to fit. If you do without gunwale cappings, the frame heads are rounded off.

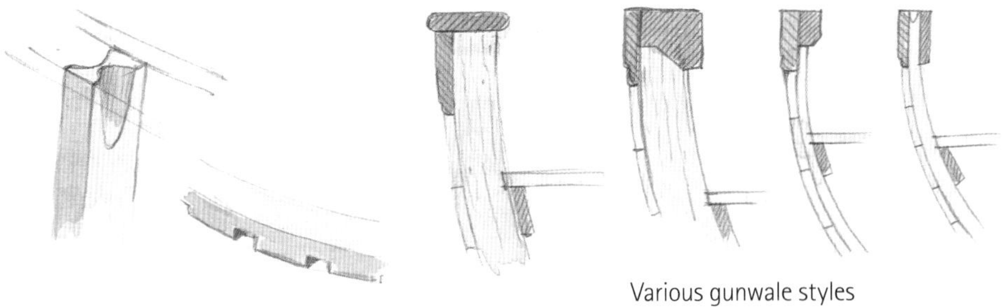

Various gunwale styles

THE KNEES

At the bows of the boat, the breasthook, cut from wood with a curved grain, helps to strengthen the inwale assembly at the stem. In the stern quarters two knees have the same function between the transom and the inwales.

Other knees are used to reinforce the risers, the partner, the centreboard casing...

Stern quarter knee

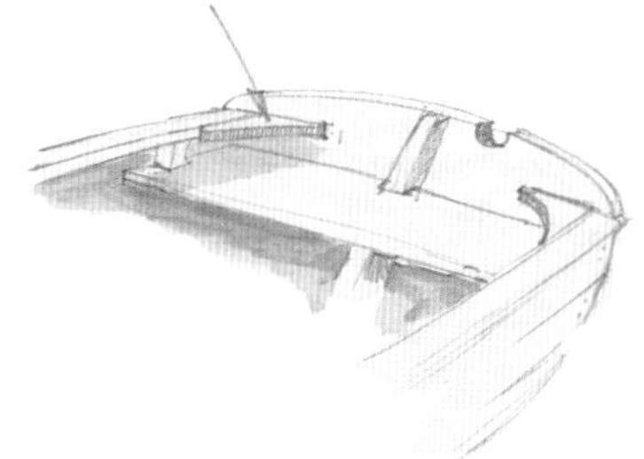

THE V-BOTTOMED HARD CHINE BOAT

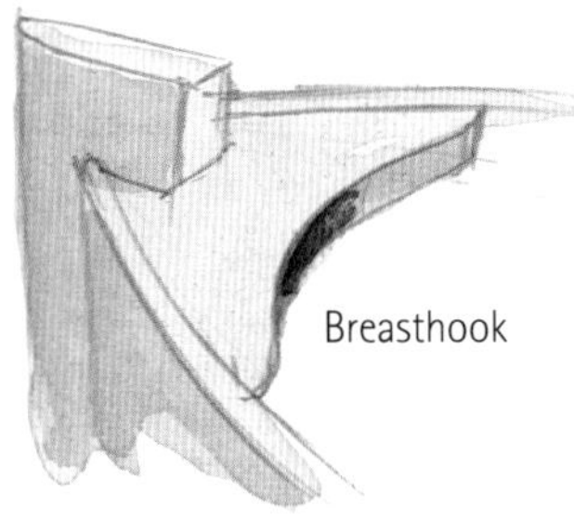

A V-bottomed hard chine boat is reinforced by a keelson set into the floors and secured with coach screws. The inwale is, as in the case of the round bilged dinghy, nailed into the futtocks, while the bilge stringer is removed: two stringers outside the frames are positioned prior to planking (page 62) and ensure the stiffness of the hull. The breasthook and stern quarter knees are identical to those of the round bilged open dinghy.

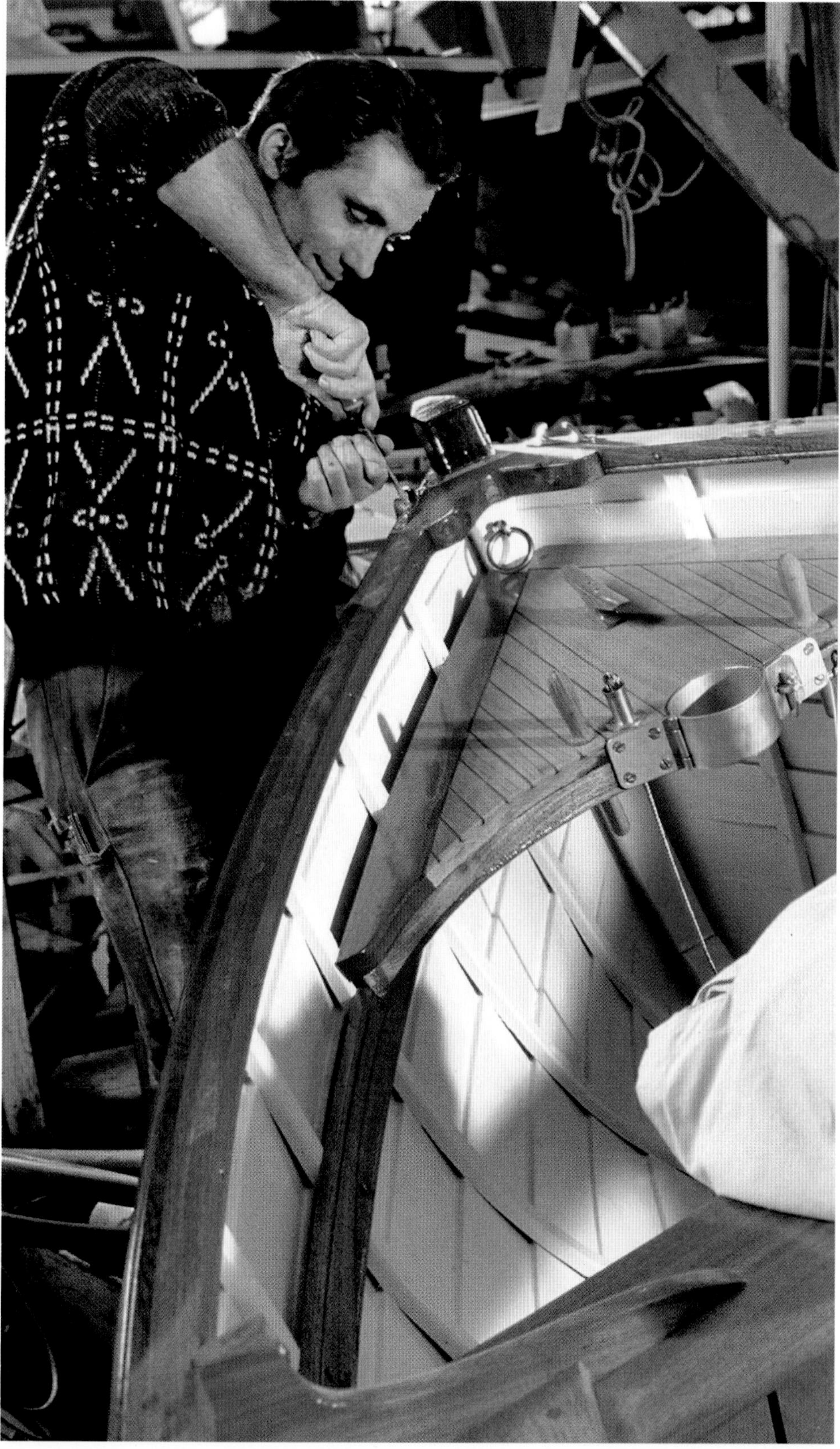

THE FLAT BOTTOMED HARD CHINE BOAT

On the flat bottomed boat, the keelson isn't necessary and a few stringers nailed onto the futtocks can add additional stiffness to the boat's bilges.

The two chines, positioned at an angle to the frame (page 63), serve as bilge stringers.

The inwale is removed and replaced by a riser situated 16cm below the sheer line. Its function, in addition to supporting the thwarts, is identical to that of an inwale.

THE RUDDER

The rudder on a traditional dinghy is made from boards of solid wood, fitted side by side with each other. They are joined together with blind metal pegs or more simply with the metal straps for the gudgeons and pintles – the hinges to let the rudder turn against the transom.

In dinghies with a centreboard, it is common to equip the rudder with a lifting blade, made either of sheet steel or plywood. The side cheeks and rudder stock are made of solid wood.

A long pintle set onto the heel of the keel make lining up and fitting the rudder easier once the boat is afloat.

THE CENTREBOARD CASE

The centreboard case is a watertight box enabling the centreboard to be contained and raised inside the boat. Above the waterline it covers the slot cut through the keel in which the centreboard swings up and down. Its assembly must be perfectly watertight and its structure solid in order to stand up to the stresses that the centreboard will place on it.

With this in mind, the case should be as compact as possible, which will be useful for the crew, because it'll take up less space in the boat and be easier to move round. The simplest case to make is one that is designed for a daggerboard. The two sides are rectangular, joined together by two uprights. The base forms a frame, carefully screwed onto the hog and made watertight by means of a polyurethane mastic glue. The top of the case, which is open, is generally supported by a thwart. A case for a pivoting centreboard is built according to the same principle, but its construction is more complex and a pivot bolt is required. Such a case always has a larger footprint than one for a daggerboard. The centreboard, which remains in the case when it is raised, is nevertheless easier to use than the daggerboard.

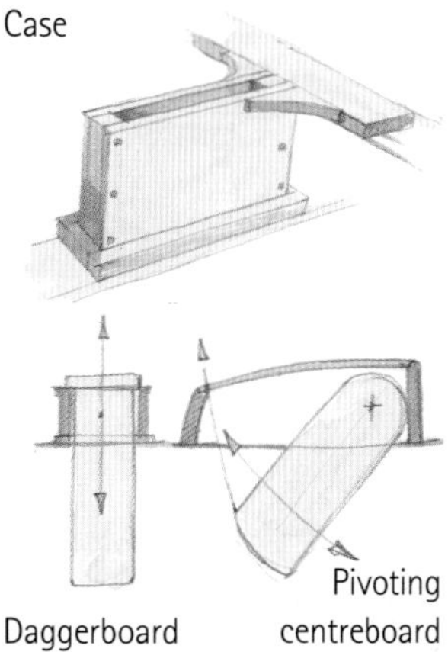

The centreboard itself can be made of edge joined boards, but is more commonly made of plywood or even sheet steel, which also gives it a secondary function as ballast.

THE DECK STRUCTURE

The presence of a deck – just like the number of masts – counts a great deal in the importance we attach to a boat. If she has a deck, you immediately consider her to be fit to brave the sea, whilst an open boat doesn't inspire such confidence. Although the presence of the deck effectively aids safety at sea, a number of open and half-deck dinghies and rowing boats have excellent seagoing qualities and can satisfy safety requirements thanks to their built-in buoyancy.

In any case, the deck is a horizontal surface covering the top of the hull and is watertight. It is supported by beams, which form part of the boat's frame and contribute to its transverse stiffness.

Half-deck dinghy

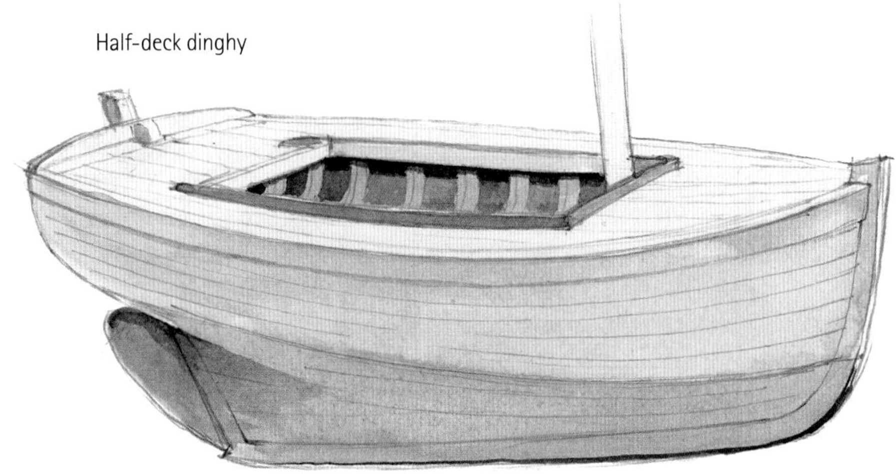

Open dinghy

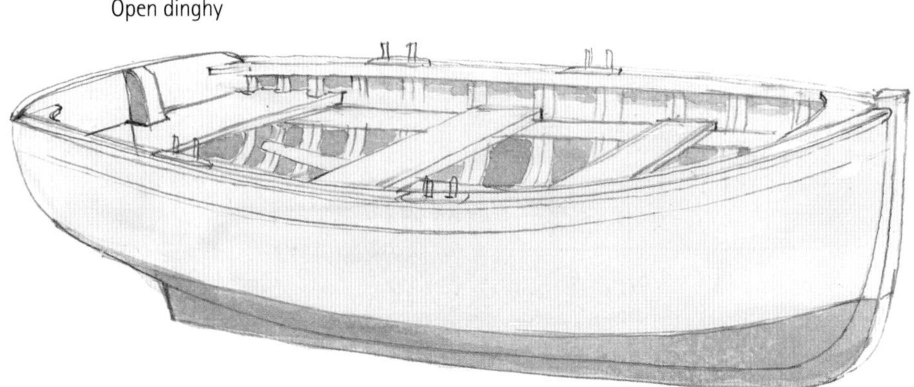

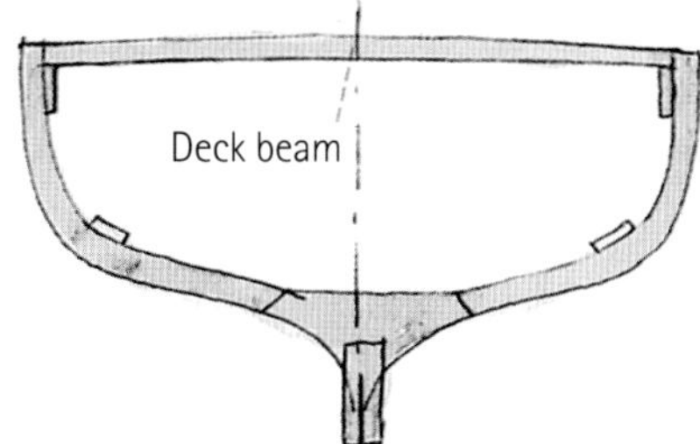

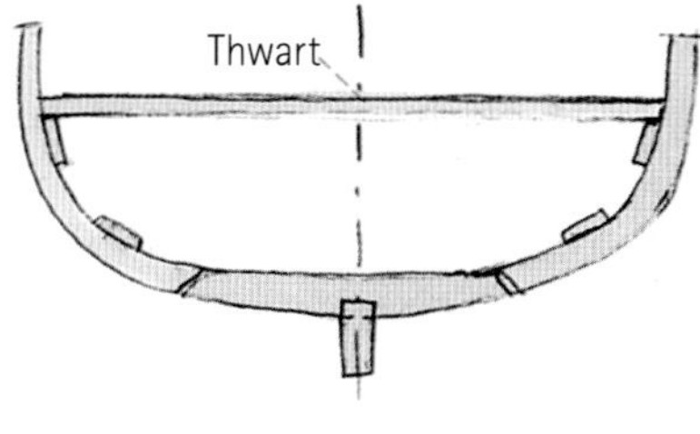

In open dinghies, the deck beams are replaced by thwarts, which aren't just simple seats, but also genuine transverse stiffeners.

The round bilged dinghy with a centreboard, the V-bottomed hard chine boat and the flat bottomed boat can all be left open, but if you favour sailing, you can add a half deck, which will leave a fairly large space in the middle of the boat for the crew. A V-bottomed hard chine boat specifically designed to sail can be decked in the same way.

On some dinghies, the fore and aft decks are fitted slightly lower down, level with the riser rather than the inwale. In such a case the inwales are joined by a large lodging knee.

THE ROUND BILGED DINGHY

The round bilged dinghy can carry fore and aft decking, linked together by two side decks, running either side of the cockpit.

THE DECK BEAMS

This assembly forms a frame joined to that of the hull. The deck beams, with their ends jointed into the inwales, run across from one side of the boat to the other, both forward and aft. To provide greater strength, they are not straight but slightly curved. They are joined to the inwale with halving joints or, better still, dovetail joints: male section at the end of the deck beam and the female section in the thickness of the inwale.

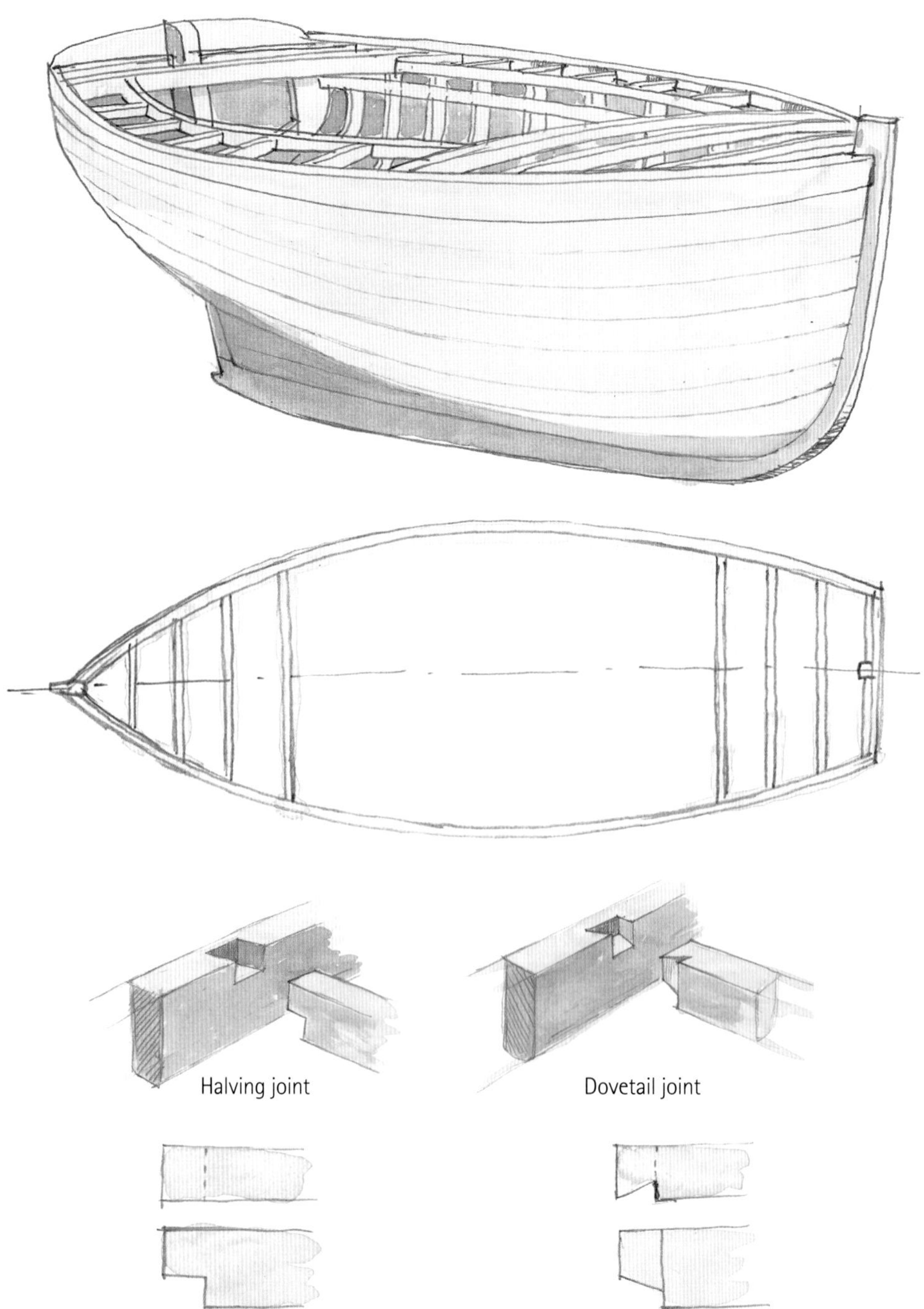

On an old boat you want to restore, it's not uncommon to find broken deck beams. With the replacement of an entire deck beam not being an easy operation, in order to make repairs you may dispense with the broken section and cut a new timber that will be scarfed in. This solution is always preferable to making a duplicate of the broken deck beam. It is worth noting that this is also true for the restoration of the majority of frame timbers.

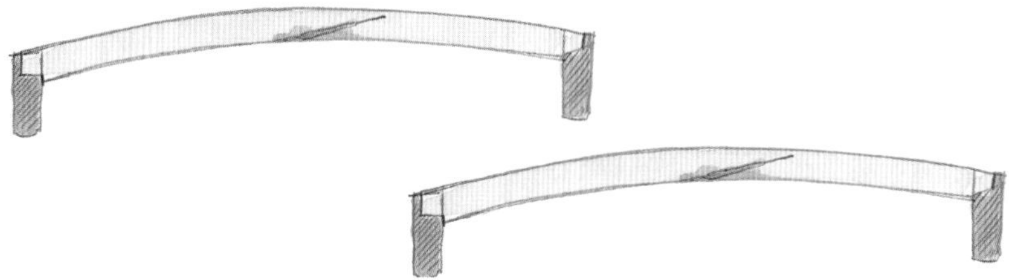

CARLINS AND HALF BEAMS

To support the side decks, two carlins join together the fore and aft decking, their ends dovetail jointed into deck beams, foreward and aft. With a cross section slightly deeper than it is wide, these timbers can be bent to follow the curve of the hull sides and will be positioned (approximately) parallel to the inwale.

Between the inwales and the carlins, half beams are assembled either side with dovetail joints.

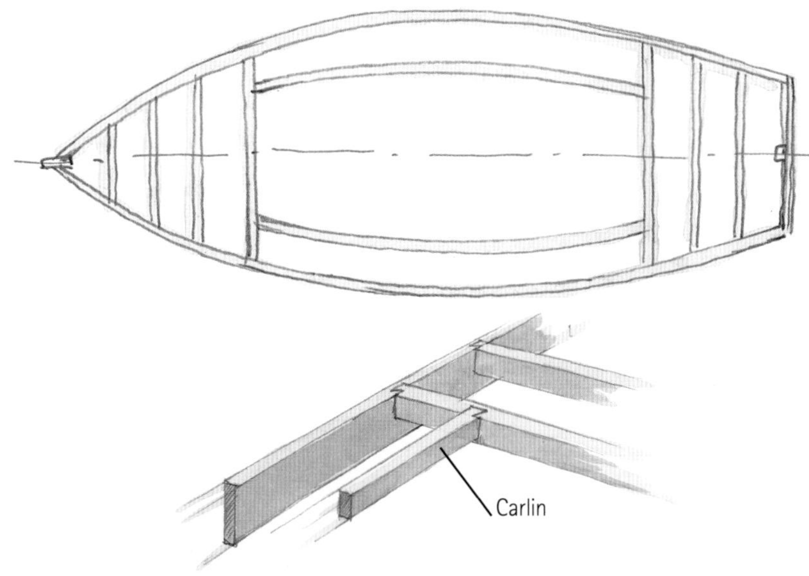

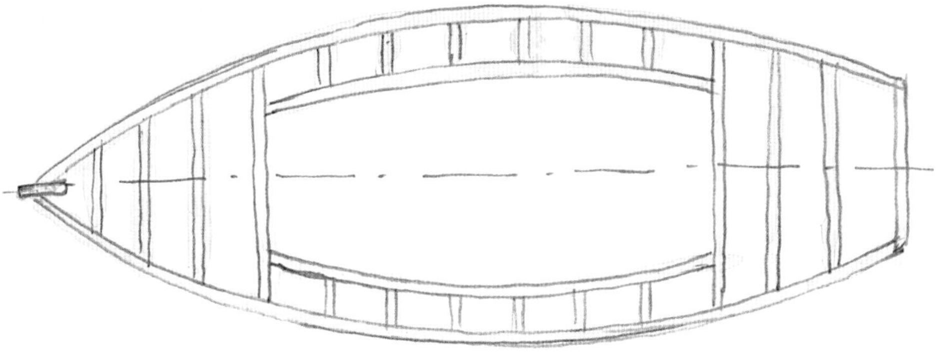

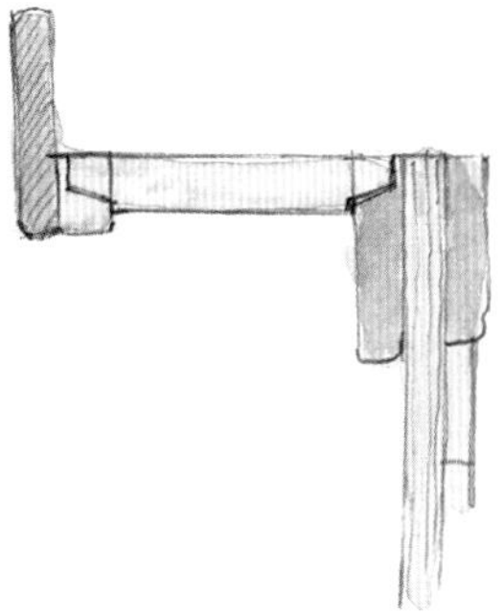

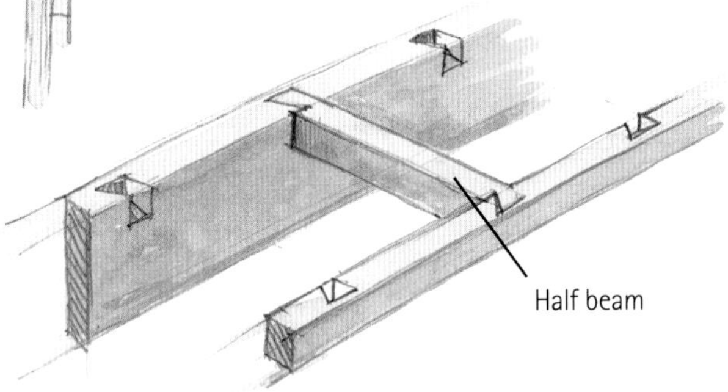

THE COCKPIT COAMING

To finish off the deck frame, a vertical coaming is added around the cockpit; it ensures the carlin has the stiffness it needs and prevents water that washes across the deck from running straight into the cockpit.

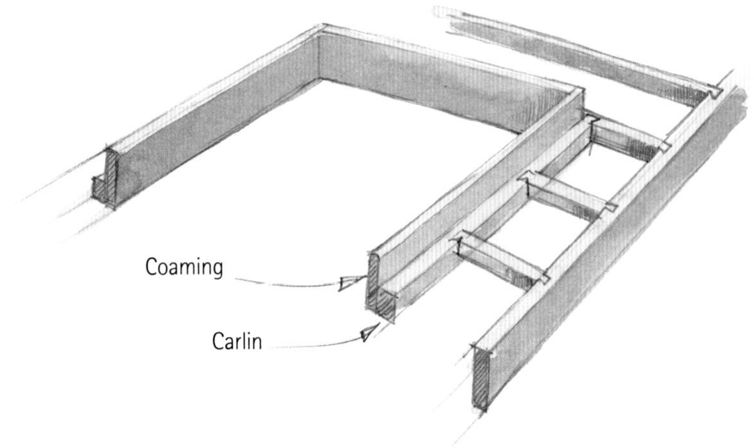

THE COVERING BOARD

Before undertaking the deck planking, you must fit the covering board. This timber, which covers the inwale, the frame or rib heads and the sheer plank, follows the hull shape. Its curved shape would, ideally, come from wood with a similar grown shape, but it is practically impossible to find such timber long enough to make the gunwale from a single piece. Consequently it will likely be made from two or three timbers scarfed together. The two covering boards need to be completely symmetrical; any variation would be particularly unsightly.

A gunwale on an open dinghy is made in the same way.

THE DECK PLANKING

Two styles of planking are common for this task. The first, which is the simpler to lay, consists of positioning straight planks edge to edge, parallel to the boat's centreline; this is the method used for the decks of work boats. However, if you wish to make this more refined and more reminiscent of the yachting look, you would opt for curved planks, laid parallel to the gunwale. Only the centreline plank (the king plank) is straight. The curved deck planks may be cut to butt against the king plank or the king plank can be notched to receive the square plank ends in a herringbone pattern. The planks, which are relatively wide to be bent laterally, are joggled into place, being laid alongside each other, the first up against the gunwale, then each against the other.

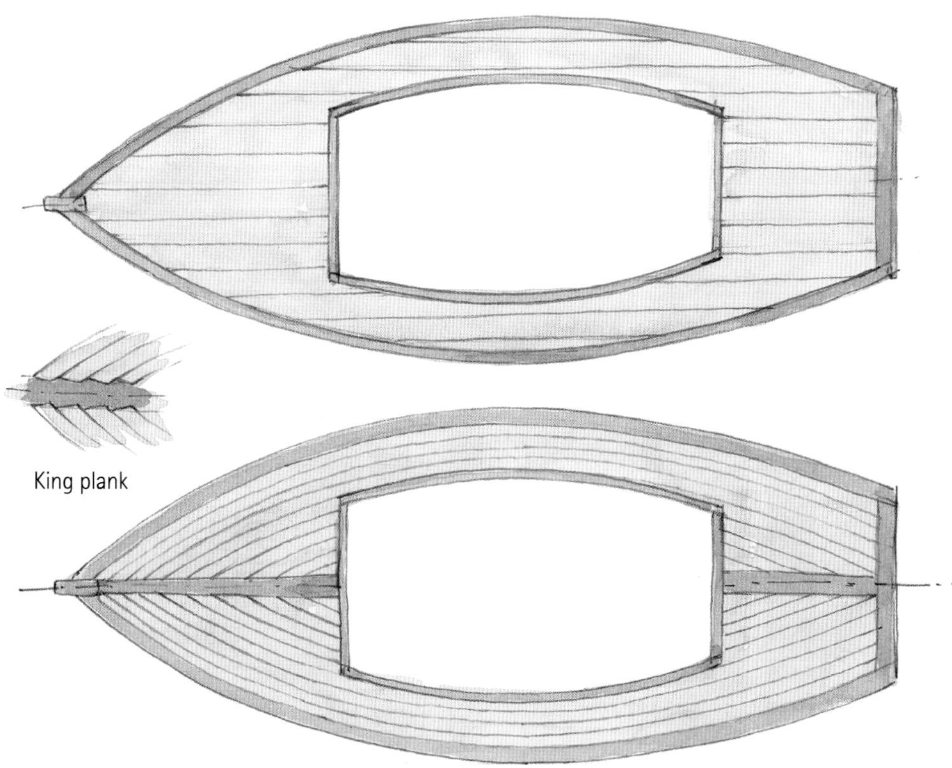

You must use numerous clamps, working slowly by screwing down the planks into the deck beams rather than nailing them; in this way the risk of breakage is reduced and the replacement, if necessary, is easier.

In days gone by, caulking of the deck was done using oakum and hot melted tar to 'pay' the seams, but today waterproof products are also used, such as polyurethane mastic, which is inserted with a mastic gun. Alternatively the deck may be covered with canvas, laid on wet paint and given a painted finish. If the deck is both payed and canvassed an excellent watertight finish is achieved.

THE RUBBING STRAKE

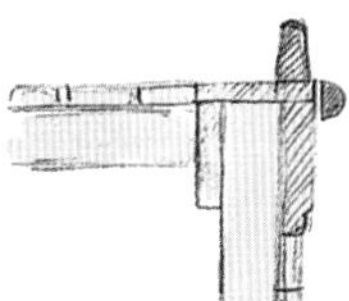

The deck-hull junction wouldn't be complete without inserting a small rubbing strake, unless the gunwale, itself rounded off and extending over the edge, substitutes for it.

The rubbing strake protects the hull, ensures watertightness between the gunwale and the sheer plank by covering the joint and also the deck canvas if the planks are laid on canvas.

THE TOE RAIL

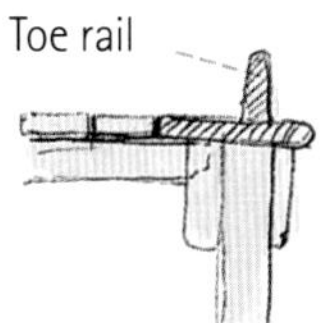

A toe rail measuring a few centimetres in height is screwed onto the top of the gunwale, along the line of the planking or very slightly set back from its edge. Scuppers, positioned at the lowest point of the sheer, prevent water from lying on the deck.

THE V-BOTTOMED HARD CHINE BOAT

Should you want decking on a V-bottomed hard chine boat, this is done in exactly the same way as on a round bilged dinghy.

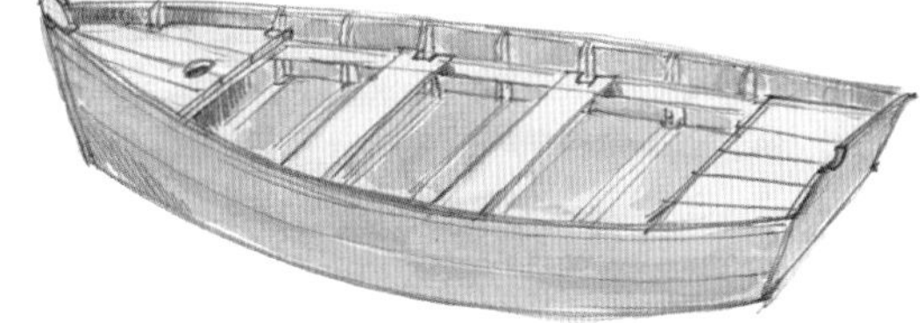

THE FLAT BOTTOMED BOAT

For the flat bottomed boat, you will be limited to a small amount of decking fore and aft, resting on top of the risers.

A PLYWOOD DECK

These days, for the sake of ease, we often make the deck from sheets of scarfed plywood, glued to the structure. This method has the benefit of ensuring watertightness and adding overall stiffness to the deck structure. For the finishing touches, the plywood can be painted, sheathed in canvas or covered by slender planking, made of straight or curved solid wood. The deck planks are then glued and screwed onto the plywood and the joint between the planks sealed using polyurethane mastic, generally black, or sometimes white if a 'yachting' finish is required.

THE ACCOMMODATION SPACE

This term refers to the internal layout of the various spaces on the boat used for navigation, living and sleeping. Generally, and although it can have a very important function, the accommodation space doesn't have a direct influence on the hull structure; it can however help to reinforce it. This is the situation with the thwarts, which constitute the main elements of the accommodation space aboard an open or half-decked dinghy, as is the case in the four examples used in this book.

THE SUPERSTRUCTURE

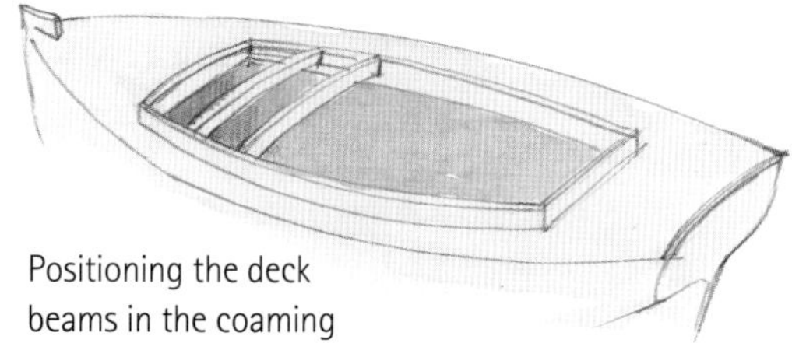

Positioning the deck beams in the coaming

The elements situated above the deck: coachroof, companionway and hatch coamings, make up the superstructure.

The four boats under discussion here are too small to carry superstructures, indeed even a cabin roof would be disproportionate.

To sleep on board, you will have to enjoy nautical camping, which essentially means stretching a sail over the cockpit, which will serve as a shelter, or you can use an over-boom cockpit cover designed specially for this purpose.

On a round bilged or V-bottomed dinghy, you may want to cover the forward section of the cockpit, without raising the coaming, so as to increase the sheltered area for stowing fishing or camping gear. However, the gains you make on the one hand are lost should you wish to settle yourself comfortably in the cockpit. Nonetheless, should you decide to stick with this option, all you have to do is add two deck beams, dovetail them into the carlins, then plank them and sheath them in canvas, as you did for the deck.

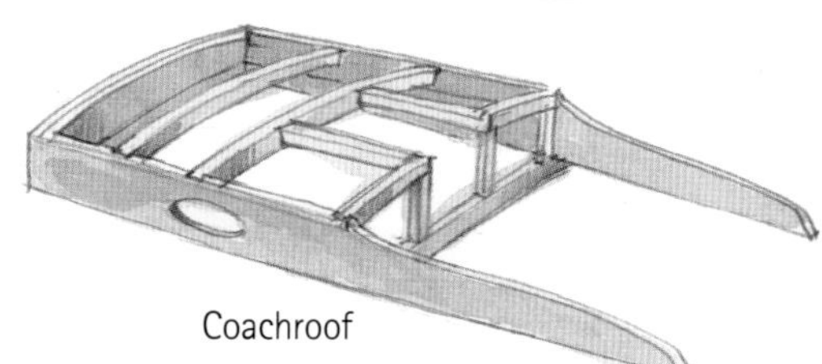

Coachroof

You will get more height in this shelter by increasing the camber of the deck beams.

For those who decide to construct a larger round bilged dinghy or V-bottomed boat - measuring 5 or 6 metres in length - a small cabin may be built with a coachroof on a slightly raised coaming. For this, the after deck beam will be cut in two to enable a hatchway to be inserted. The two half beams are supported by the bulkhead uprights and two carlins joining onto the central beam.

If the hatch is hinged, you will have to make provision for a coaming around the opening, extending forward via two runners if the hatch is a sliding one.

PROTECTING WOODEN HULLS

The finish of a wooden hull and its later maintenance, come down to one main operation: painting. By this we mean all kinds of paints, varnish or protection products.

When the hull is new, you begin by the impregnation of all the timbers with red-lead paint. Only the woodwork to be varnished escapes this rule. It is desirable to paint the frame timbers as the construction progresses, which will prevent the wood from drying out and cracking. Special care must be taken with any wood that will be hidden by other timbers.

The planking is painted with a first coat as soon as possible for the same reasons as before: red lead paint for the areas to be painted, diluted varnish for any wood to be varnished.

For the finishing touches, three or four coats of paint will be essential. The first is slightly diluted, then the others are applied undiluted, in dry weather and sheltered from strong sunlight. You must use paints that are sufficiently flexible to accept the expansion and contraction of the wood due to variations in heat and humidity: one pack polyurethane paint (you reserve two pack epoxy or polyurethane for boats planked with unsheathed strip-planking or plywood, which are more stable materials). Pitch is highly economical and ensures excellent protection, so it was a good choice for fishing craft that were very simple in design. An initial coat composed of a mixture of pitch and liquid tar provided the best wood conservation.

Sanding the paint (with the exception of pitch) between each coat is essential. Done with wet and dry, it enables you to key the surface in preparation for the next coat.

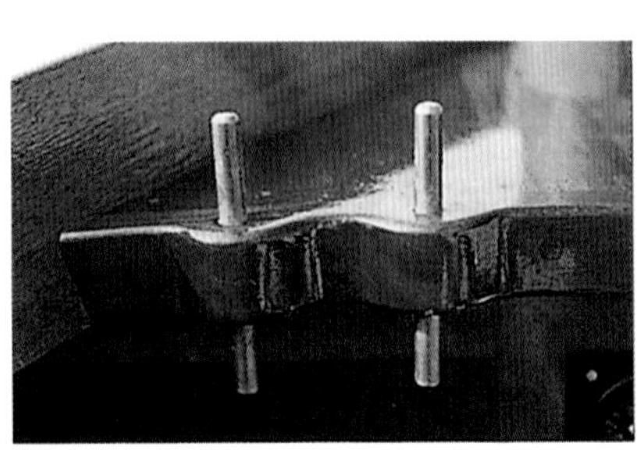

Varnishing is done in the same conditions, that is, in dry weather with sanding, but there will be more coats: at least seven or eight coats.

A few products aimed at protection and penetration are easier to apply and require little or no sanding between coats: these are called stains. Their silky appearance can be quite flattering, but cannot rival a real varnish. You can also resort to Norwegian tar, which is particularly well suited to wooden boats, as well as more modern products such as penetrating oils with surface drying capabilities.

Below the waterline, underwater paints or 'antifouling' don't involve any particular application problems. However, small boats, which are generally lifted out of the water after each day's sailing, will not be treated with this type of paint. Their bilge is painted with the same paint or varnish as thc rcst of the hull.

The choice of colours is a matter of taste. However, it is advisable to remain understated if you want to retain the spirit of traditional boats: white, pitch, blue, green, red, grey. You just have to look around you and follow the example of the pretty little craft dotted around the port.

MAINTENANCE

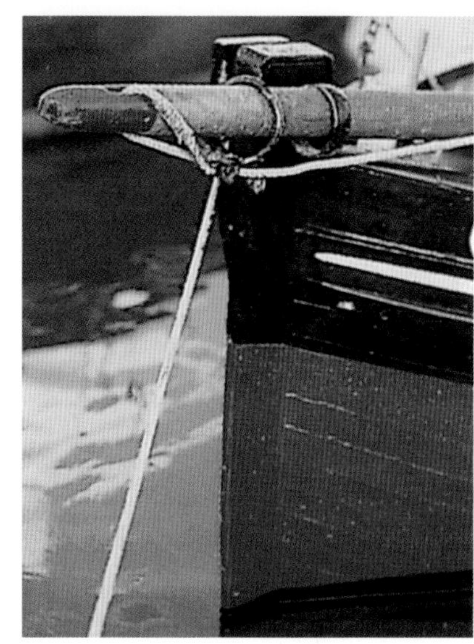

If the protection of the hull has been done carefully from when the boat was built, maintenance will be considerably easier. Each year it is sufficient, at the start of the season, to sand the surface coat, focusing particular attention on the places that have suffered wear, impact and scrapes. The latter form the subject of a first coat of red lead or primer and an undercoat in the colour of the hull. After sanding these touch-ups, the whole of the hull can be given a new top coat.

For varnishes, you proceed in the same way: general sanding, localised touch-ups. If the wood has turned black you must apply a special product designed to give it back its original colour. This product requires abundant rinsing. You begin with a localised touch-up with diluted varnish (one or several coats) and you end by brushing on one or two coats over the whole boat.

Hulls that have had pitch applied don't require sanding, but rather a vigorous brushing off and a wash. Once the touch-ups have been applied, a single coat will be necessary over the whole boat.

Old antifouling is cleaned by scraping away the underwater dirt, brushing and washing, if possible using a pressure washer. You must never dry sand this highly toxic paint. You make do with applying a fresh coat over the cleaned surface.

Take the opportunity, during this process, to check the condition of any metal parts and particularly the planking nails. Any suspicious area is immediately brushed down so as to remove any traces of corrosion, then protected by a phosphate paint, red lead or zinc paint according to its compatibility with the original treatment (black steel or galvanised steel). The nail heads treated in this way have filler applied to them and are touched up prior to a final coat of paint. The same applies to any metal fittings: chainplates, pintles, gudgeons.

THE RIG

Everything that's above the deck and necessary for sailing and manoeuvring the boat or keeping the masts and spars up, forms the rig: masts, yards, spars, shrouds, sails, halyards, sheets, etc. You also use this word to designate a type of sail area or a suit of sails. As such you refer to: a lugger rig, a gaff rig, a lateen rig, or on a dinghy a dipping lug rig, sloop, cutter, etc. Here we will solely be discussing rigs for small boats.

MASTS AND SPARS

To make masts and spars for traditional boats, you would opt for coniferous trees whose trunks display enough resistance and flexibility to be used without any preparation other than simple planing designed to achieve a round, smooth shape.

SOLID MASTS

These are traditional masts, which are strong but fairly heavy and are best suited to boats which themselves have a fairly strong hull. This is generally true of local, traditional boats. Different species of tree can be used: locally sourced pine, European larch, Baltic redwood, Scots pine, Red fir and spruce. Avoid the knot rings that are the source of weak points.

If you're after a more refined mast, which is perfectly cylindrical, it will be necessary to start out with a tree whose diameter is considerably larger than that of the planned mast and then plane it down to get rid of any natural warping. You will have to do the same with the length, because the top of the tree doesn't generally have enough stiffness.

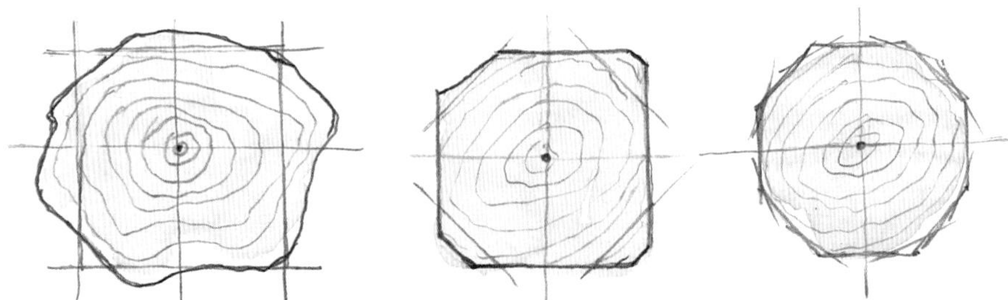

To begin this job, you plane four flat sides, regularly checking it with a square, a ruler and a line. From that square form, the corners are planed down so that you have an octagonal section. From the octagonal you plane the corners off, and so on until a circular section is achieved. Sometimes it is necessary to plane for a long time so as to get rid of any irregularities in the trunk.

Little by little the circle takes shape; the rest will be achieved through sanding and finishing off.

You will notice that the mast of a gaff rigged boat is cylindrical along the greater part of its length and will be completed by lightly tapering it above the hounds for the shrouds; this top part is referred to as the topmast. On a mast without shrouds, as is generally the case on a boat with a lug rig, the reduction in diameter is more gradual; it begins halfway down its length.

SOLID OR HOLLOW MASTS MADE FROM DEAL

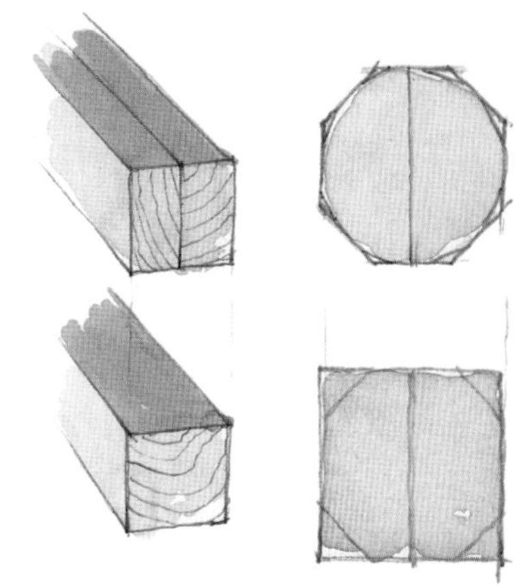

Today, the wooden masts of small boats are often manufactured from deal cut in a sawmill. You glue two thick rectangular deal planks one against the other, so as to get a square section with increased stiffness (compared with that of a single deal plank of the same cross section).

In fact, the grain of a square beam is rarely perfectly straight and part of the grain will be cut, whereas the two thick deal planks will tend to make up for their individual weaknesses.

For large masts, you cannot obtain planks from a single length of wood, so it's necessary to join them together with scarfs beforehand and then stick them together after placing them on trestles that are nicely in line. For this gluing they will be pressed together using clamps positioned around every 20cm. From this square section it will be easy to obtain eight sides, then 16 and so on.

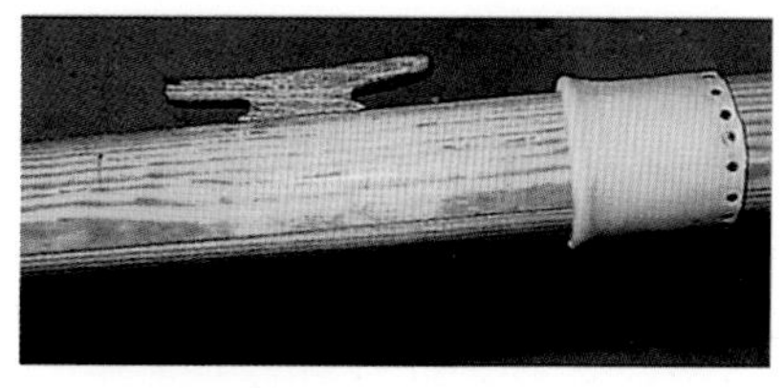

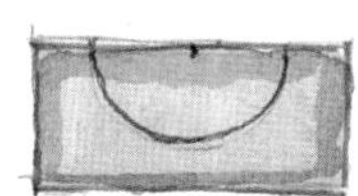

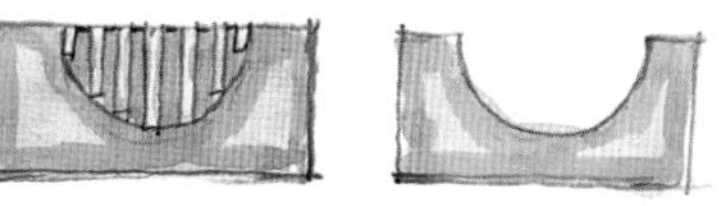

Making a mast from two thick deal planks also enables it to be made lighter in weight by hollowing it out before gluing. This work can be done using a circular saw, adjusted to varying depths of cut, the remaining strips being removed with a wood chisel. The interior surface will be finished off with a gouge, or better still with the help of a plane with a curved sole. The mast foot, the masthead and the sections at the hounds and other fittings are left solid.

The hollowed out parts culminate in a cone shape to avoid break points, as shown on the right.

If the mast includes a groove for the sail's bolt rope (which may be the case for small yachts with a Bermudan rig), you hollow out each side of the groove with a gouge or a rabbet plane (grooved plane), prior to gluing. In this case, the mast section is left slightly oval across the back so as to maintain enough surface area for adhesion.

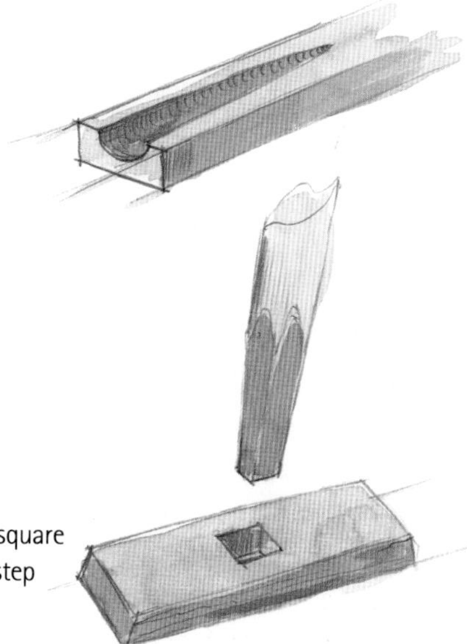

THE MAST FOOT AND PARTNERS

The bottom end of the mast is cut into the shape of a tenon, so that it can be fitted into the mast step, which is attached to the boat's keel or keelson. The mast step on small craft with a lugger rig is simply cut into a square, tapering off the further down it goes. The mast goes through the partners, a hole made in the deck or in a thwart, which also ensures it is supported.

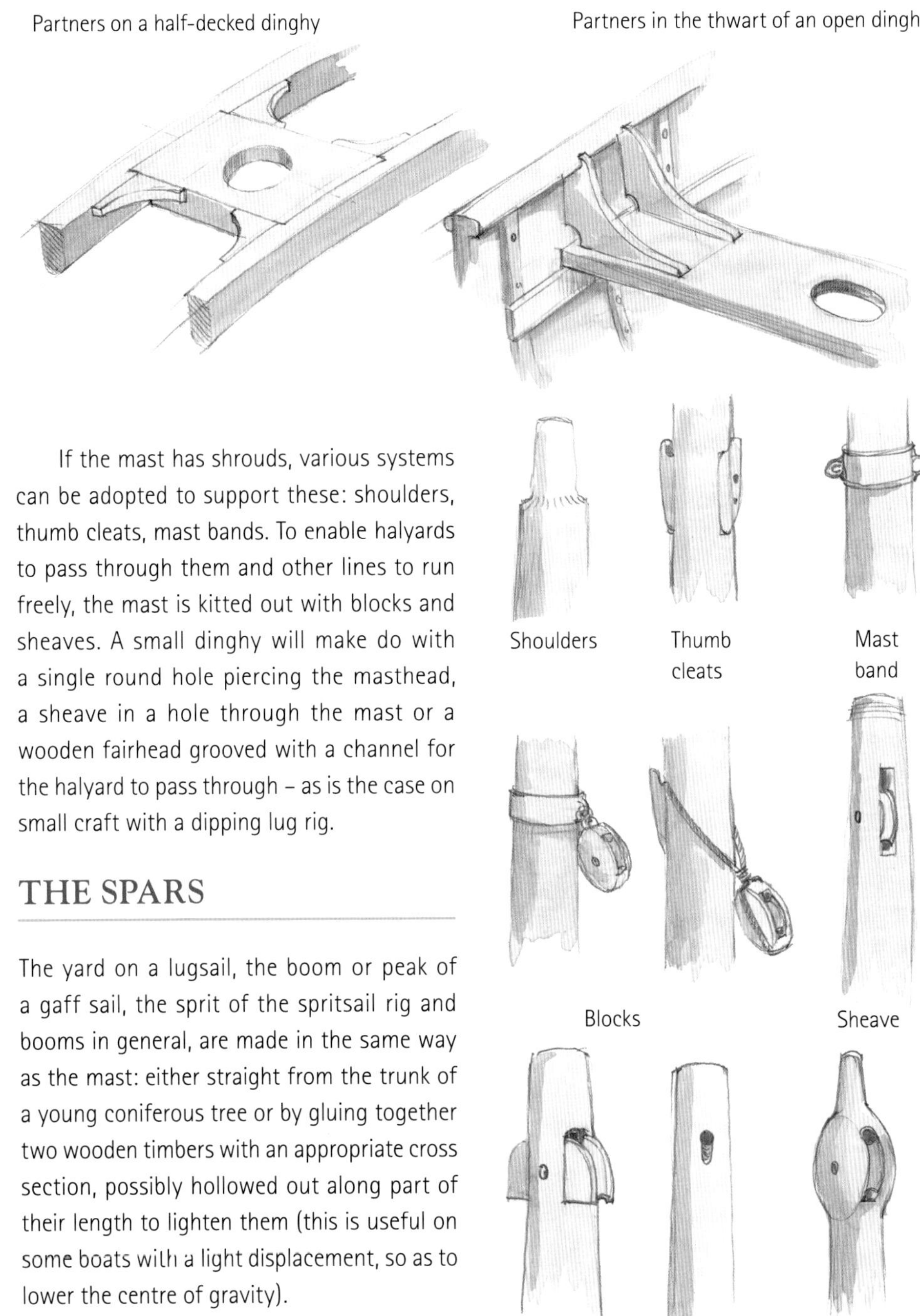

If the mast has shrouds, various systems can be adopted to support these: shoulders, thumb cleats, mast bands. To enable halyards to pass through them and other lines to run freely, the mast is kitted out with blocks and sheaves. A small dinghy will make do with a single round hole piercing the masthead, a sheave in a hole through the mast or a wooden fairhead grooved with a channel for the halyard to pass through – as is the case on small craft with a dipping lug rig.

THE SPARS

The yard on a lugsail, the boom or peak of a gaff sail, the sprit of the spritsail rig and booms in general, are made in the same way as the mast: either straight from the trunk of a young coniferous tree or by gluing together two wooden timbers with an appropriate cross section, possibly hollowed out along part of their length to lighten them (this is useful on some boats with a light displacement, so as to lower the centre of gravity).

Certain booms carry a groove, identical to that of the mast, to accommodate the sail's bolt rope. Each of these spars has, at each end, a system enabling the sail outhauls to be attached, which involves a simple hole or groove, or sometimes a small fitting. The articulation and joint with the mast require a notch for the spritsail rig and jaws for gaff rigs. The jaws are made from hardwood with a perfectly straight grain.

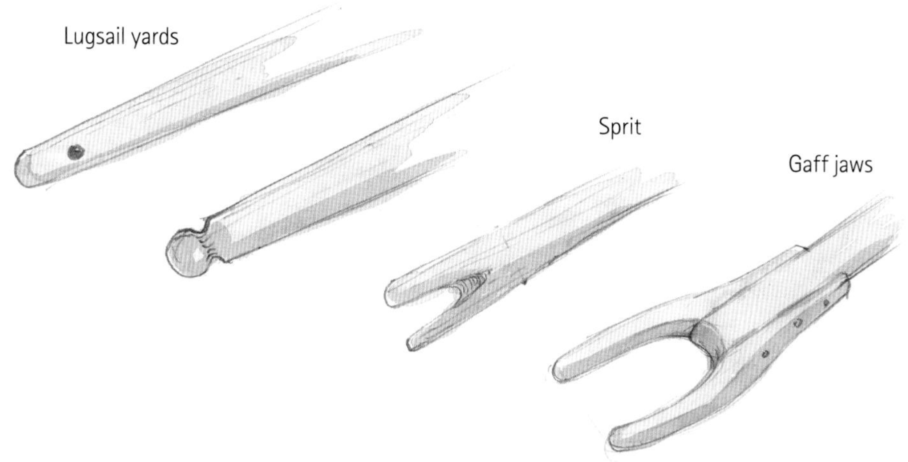

RUNNING RIGGING AND STANDING RIGGING

The running rigging, which serves to set the sails and control them, uses rope that used to be made from hemp or cotton, but is today more commonly made from synthetic fibres, some of which look quite like natural rope.

On small boats, the running rigging is generally limited to halyards and sheets, to which, on larger craft, you can add topping lifts, brails, reefing pennants and boom vangs. These ropes require simple finishing and rope work, which is within the scope of the amateur: whipping, splicing, flat or racking seizing.

Small craft with either a lugsail or sprit rig usually have free-standing masts without standing rigging (no shrouds, forestay or backstay). When they're gaff rigged, they often have a pair of shrouds on each side and a forestay, occasionally accompanied by runners (running backstays). The standing rigging of yachts with Bermudan rigs is completed by cap shrouds extending up to the masthead and backstays aft.

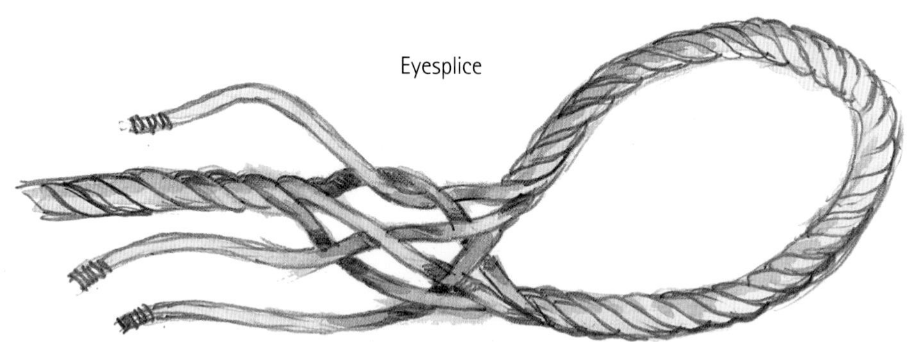

To make eyes and loops in wire rope, rather than hand splicing them, we now commonly use swaged terminals made by professionals with the help of powerful presses. It's a shame because though the classic wire splice requires strength and expertise, swaged terminals are a lot easier to make and just as strong.

In small diameter wire rope it's possible to turn in a simple eyesplice (known as a Portuguese eyesplice) by separating the strands into two groups, for example four strands on one side, three on the other, then crossing them over and relaying the strands up each side of the eye, filling in the empty gaps in the laid parts.

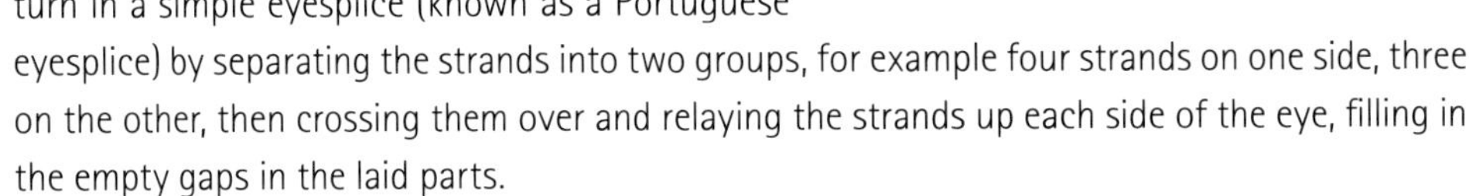

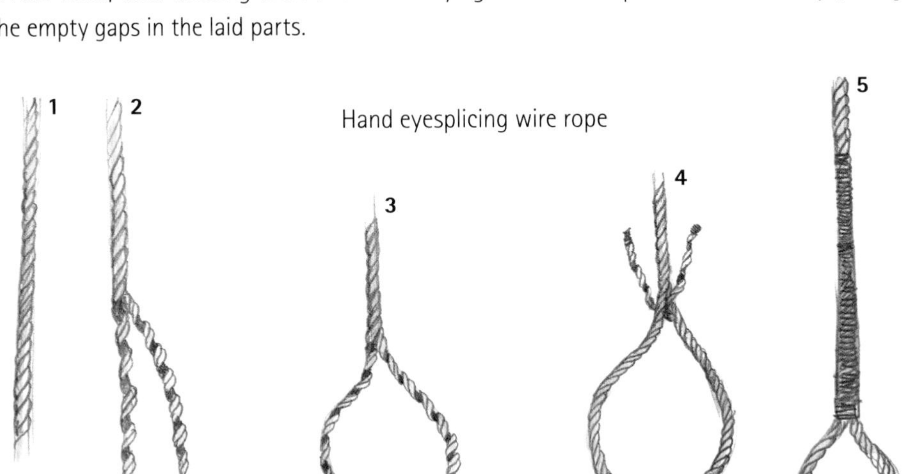

Hand eyesplicing wire rope

You can, alternatively, place a series of three very tight seizings on the wire to form an eye, which is also strong.

Seizing

SAILS

The rigs on traditional yachts show the same diversity as their hull shapes and construction methods do. They vary according to region and port, the function for which they were designed, or according to local tradition. We will not cover large three-masted vessels with square sails, not luggers, but rather we will look at a few of the simplest rig possibilities that can be used on small boats.

Lug rig

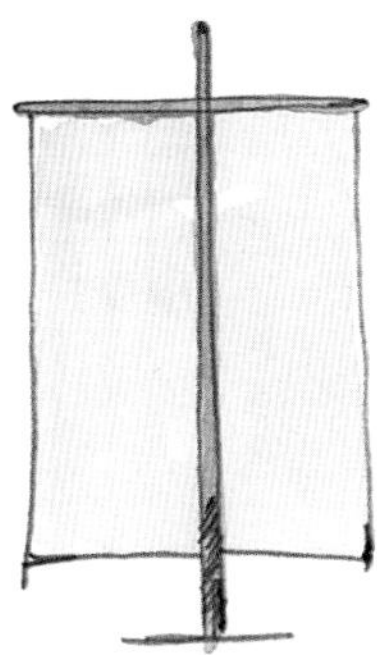

THE SQUARE SAIL

This is the oldest sail of all, having been used in very ancient times as well as later on board Viking ships. More recently it powered the square riggers that traded the world's oceans and it can still be found today on a few rare replicas and sail training ships. It works on all points of sail, but is most effective in downwind conditions, such as the world's trade winds. Its weaknesses are in sailing close-hauled and when tacking.

THE LUGSAIL

Originally identical to a square sail, but with the yard moved aft to place the mast about a third of the way back from the leading edge, the lugsail gradually took on a geometry of its own. The yard was tilted upwards, its overall shape tending more towards a triangle, and its capabilities when beating to windward were greatly improved. However, when tacking, one tack is slightly less favourable than the other, because the sail ends up flat against the mast and loses a little of its effectiveness. When there is a large section forward of the mast you can 'dip' the lug during a tack, which means switching the yard and sail across to leeward side of the mast.

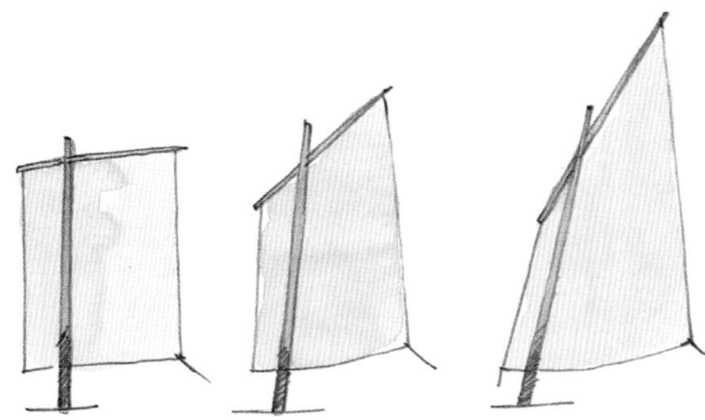

THE GAFF SAIL

Situated entirely abaft (behind) the mast, on which it pivots, the gaff sail is supported by a spar – the gaff – attached to the mast with a set of jaws serving as a pivot. It has the ability to beat into the wind equally well on both tacks. However, it's on downwind points of sail that the gaff sail shows its true power and is particularly effective.

Some gaff mainsails are very high peaked, to the extent that they're on the point of becoming triangular, the peak practically extending to the top of the mast: these sails are referred to as a gunter sail.

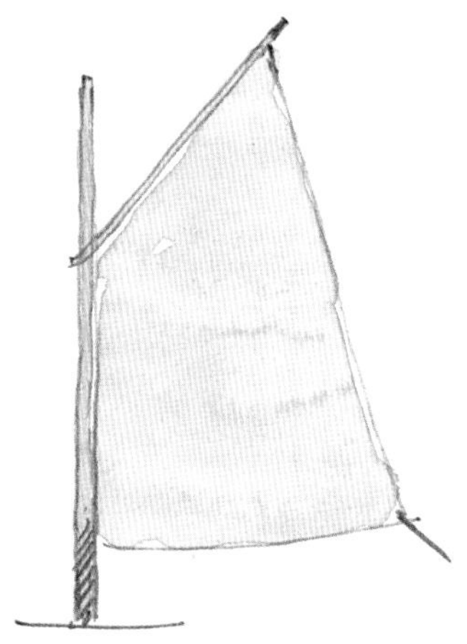

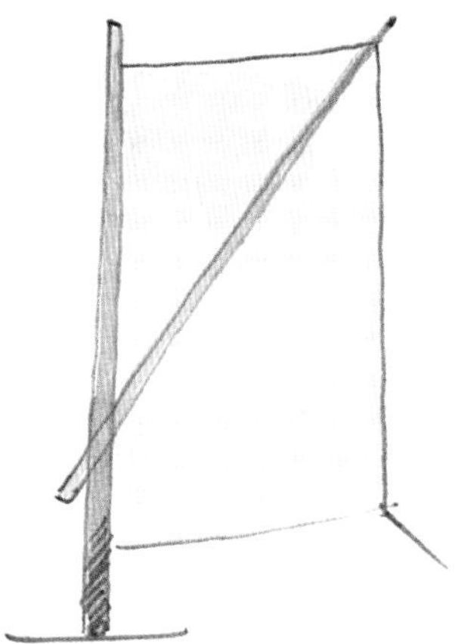

SPRITSAIL

Like the gaff rig, the spritsail is hoisted with the luff abaft the mast; it is supported by a diagonally positioned spar: the sprit.

THE BERMUDAN SAIL

Triangular in shape, carried on a tall mast, the Bermudan sail doesn't have a peak or a yard. It's excellent for beating; however it does require fairly complicated shrouds to support the mast. This type of rig, which is seldom used on traditional boats, is carried on numerous small classic yachts and the majority of light keelboats. It is unsuitable for a working boat in which it may be necessary to be able to reduce the rig and due to the height of the mast.

The term 'gaff sail' is often used incorrectly to describe any trapezoidal sail with a yard, including lug sails and sprit sails.

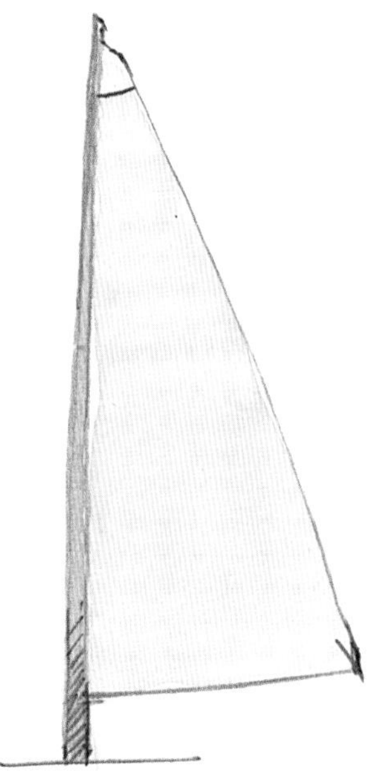

THE MAIN TYPES OF RIG

On small dinghies, classic yachts and small working boats, the most frequently used rigs, with all their variations, are those of the sloop, the cutter, the cutter rigged yawl, dipping lug...

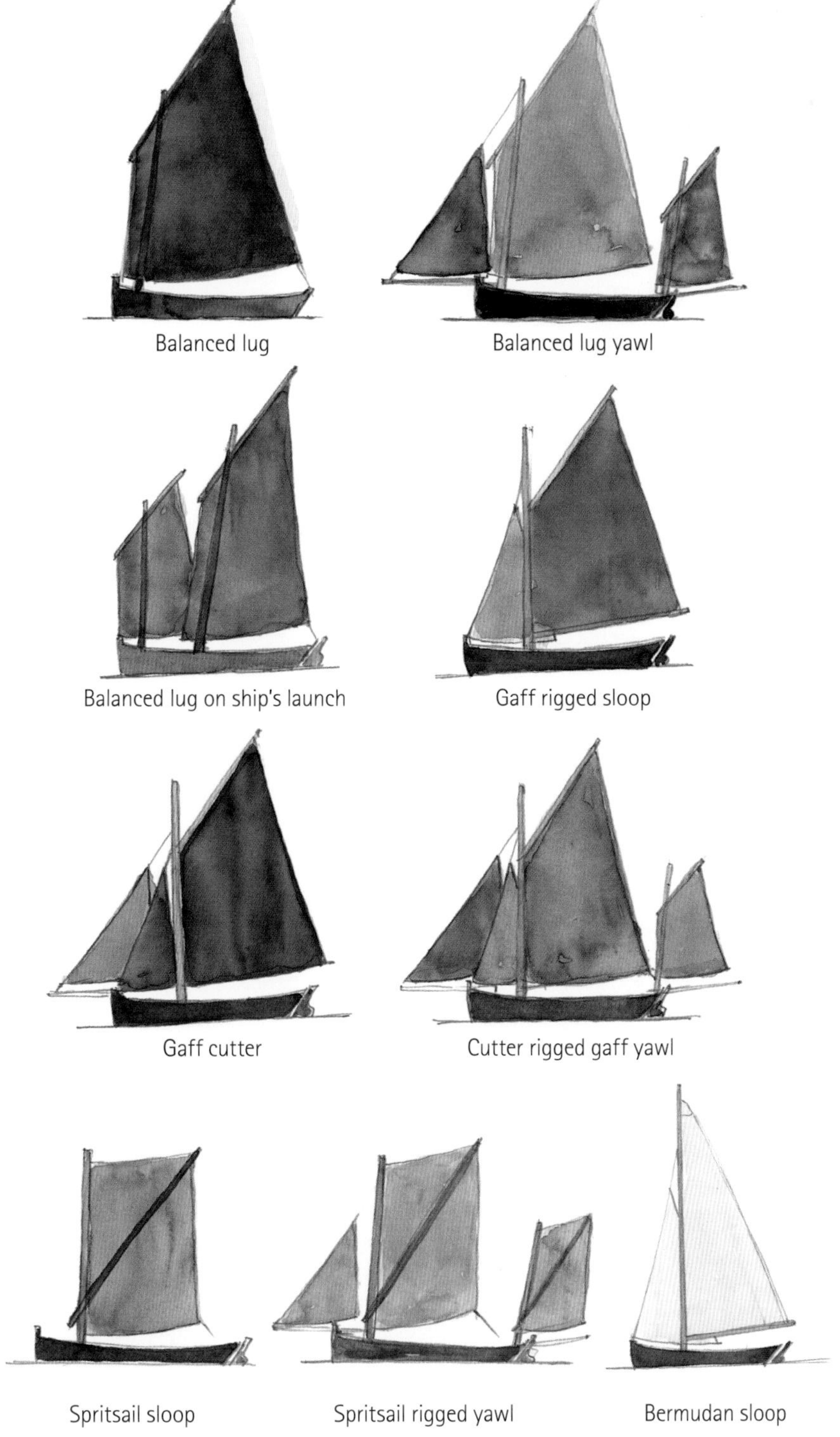

Balanced lug

Balanced lug yawl

Balanced lug on ship's launch

Gaff rigged sloop

Gaff cutter

Cutter rigged gaff yawl

Spritsail sloop

Spritsail rigged yawl

Bermudan sloop

SAILMAKING

It is often claimed that sails made by an amateur inevitably lead to wretched results. While this may be true for a large boat, it is not necessarily the case for a small craft. It's obvious that the skills of the sailmaker, who works with a flexible, stretchy material, are harder to master (although it depends who's learning) than the carpentry skills needed to make a wooden frame, whose shape no longer varies once the wood is shaped.

Undoubtedly, being used to the processes plays a role: although the majority of amateur boatbuilders entrust the making of their sails to a sailmaker, it is possible to attempt to make a small sail yourself. Perhaps it won't be faultless, but at least it will enable trials to be made and should give you the chance to go sailing for very little cost.

You will use the simplest method – the flat cut – which has long been used for sailing craft as well as being used by sailor-fishermen in days when they sewed the sails of a small craft themselves.

For this you would choose a mixed fabric (synthetic and cotton) without a coating, which is close woven and not too heavy. Whatever the width of the canvas, we will cut vertical strips – the panels – from 40 to 50cm (work things out to the minimum to avoid wasting canvas).

The sail shape is drawn out at full scale on a perfectly clean board. The sides are marked out with string and chalk allowing 15cm extra on each edge for finishing. To make things simple, you will ensure that the luff and leech are straight. You will add 5 per cent to produce camber in the foot.

Outline with string

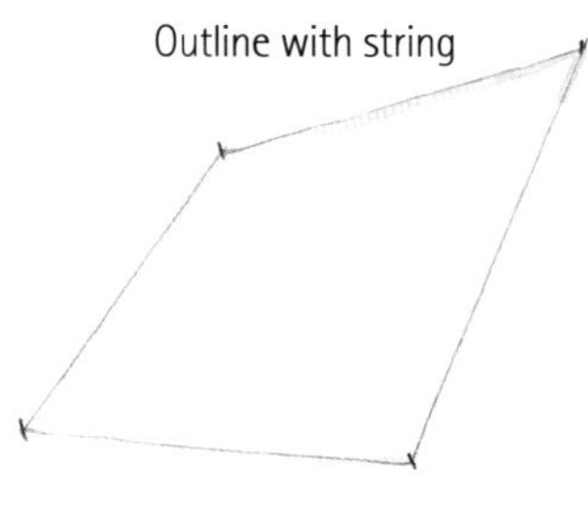

Camber of the foot

Positioning of the panels

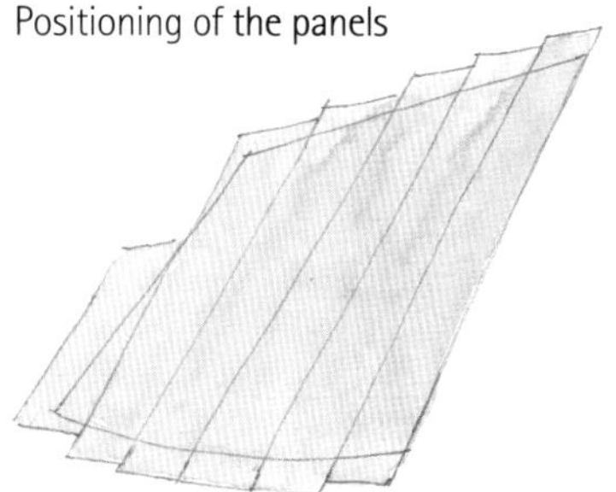

On this plan, the canvas panels are extended parallel to the leech, by overlapping them across 4cm (2cm either side of the fold, after the seam is turned down). These panels are numbered and then joined one onto the other, either by making a flat seam stitch bound by hand (a fairly laborious job though the results are very strong), or using a zigzag stitch with a sewing machine. Once all the panels are gathered together, the whole thing is put back flat on the floor and the excess at the edges (15cm) is cut away: these sections will be used to make the tablings. Before making the latter, you position reinforcements in the corners of the sail; these are formed from several thicknesses of fabric, positioned and sewn together with a binding stitch or a zigzag stitch, as will be the case for the tablings.

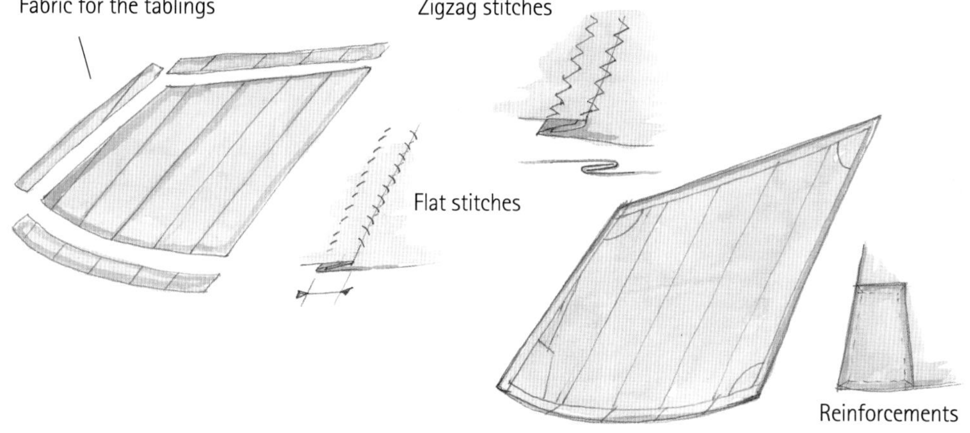

SETTING THE BOLT ROPE ON

The bolt rope is made of tarred hemp or an imitation synthetic rope. Setting the bolt rope on, which consists of sewing a reinforcing rope (the bolt rope) around the edge of the sail is a relatively tricky operation. Indeed you have to tension this bolt rope so that it is neither too tight nor too loose, to avoid making some horrible folds appear in the sail. The best thing is to tension the sail between two points, then in turn tension the bolt rope more forcefully between these two points. The difference in tension is spread across its length via successive stitches, starting with the middle, then the quarter, then the eighth, etc. Finally, the bolt rope is sewn permanently along its entire length, progressing from left to right, stitching between the strands of the rope.

Another less orthodox method consists of replacing the bolt rope with a flat tape sewn along the edge of the sail beneath the tabling.

On small sails it is pointless sewing a bolt rope along the leech and head – just the foot and the luff need to be roped.

For the finishing touches, a few tapes, cringles (small holes pierced into the reef band near the bolt ropes) and reef points will be needed, these last being sewn directly into the edges of the panels.

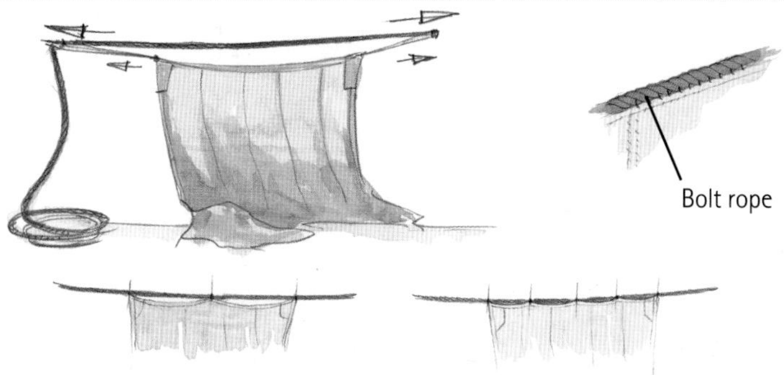

TANNING SAILS

The sails of traditional craft may be tanned. This operation protects the cotton against mildew and gives it a beautiful colour. For example, ochre powder is used, which will be mixed with very hot (but not boiling) water, using 1kg of powder for every 10 litres, and you then add half a litre of linseed oil to the mix. The spent tanbark is applied with a scrubbing brush on both sides of the sail, which is laid flat on a smooth surface. You can also use a less customary method that provides good results: this consists of replacing the linseed oil with white vinyl glue (wood glue), using 500 grams for every 10 litres; the work will then be carried out using a cold water mix.

MAINTAINING THE SAILS

After each season, the sails are carefully rinsed, dried and put away, especially if they're made of cotton.

You then proceed with checking the stitches and repairing the seams, eyelets, cringles, etc. In the first fine days of spring, a spent tanbark mixture can be made up if the sail is made from cotton, to give it back its colour and its protection.

PRACTICAL INFORMATION

AMATEUR CONSTRUCTION

Amateur construction is a real adventure. To help the builder go through the various stages from the decision about which design to build, to the launch of the boat, some practical information is provided here: boatbuilding courses; a bibliography listing some useful books on boatbuilding and magazines that cover the subject; regulations; and because you need to know how to express yourself in 'nautical' terms, a glossary of some construction and general nautical terms.

BOATBUILDING COURSES

This book is for amateur builders who are predominantly self-taught, observing the boats around them, gathering information from books and articles published in boating magazines and gleaning practical boatbuilding information from a variety of sources. However, there is a big difference between theory and practice and while many will be happy just to learn from their (inevitable) mistakes, others will prefer to invest in a practical course on boatbuilding of which there are a number available in the UK.

Courses in practical boatbuilding are offered at the following centres:

Boat Building Academy, Monmouth Beach, Lyme Regis, Dorset DT7 3JN
Tel: 01297 445545
www.boatbuildingacademy.com
38-week course in boatbuilding, maintenance and support to City & Guilds Level 3; 1-5 day short courses in specific aspects of boat building, woodworking and related skills which can be structured to a student's specific requirements.

Falmouth Marine School, Admissions Office, University College, Woodlane, Falmouth, Cornwall TR11 4RH
Tel: 01326 310310
www.college-falmouth.ac.uk
35-week course in yacht fit out and composites City & Guilds Level 3.

International Boat Building Training College, Sea Lake Road, Oulton Broad, Lowestoft, Suffolk NR32 3LQ
Tel: 01502 569663
www.ibtc.co.uk
47-week diploma course in boatbuilding with option of City & Guilds Levels 2/3; 3-4 day course in lofting; 1-day course in caulking.

Nottage Maritime Institute, The Quay, Wivenhoe, Colchester, Essex CO7 9BX
Tel: 01206 824142
http://homepages.rya-online.net/nottage-maritime-institute/
The Nottage Institute runs a traditional clinker boatbuilding course over weekends. Students build their own traditional Nottage clinker dinghy which takes a total of 400 to 500 hours to complete, spread over a few years. Consideration is given to those who wish to construct a boat other than the traditional Nottage dinghy.

Pembrokeshire College, Haverfordwest, Pembrokeshire SA61 1SZ
Tel: 0800 716236, 01437 753000
www.pembrokeshire.ac.uk
2-year full time City & Guilds Boatbuilding

In addition, a number of further education colleges throughout the country offer City and Guilds courses, either full-time or part-time, in boatbuilding and related skills.

BIBLIOGRAPHY

Readers of this book may also find one or more of the following books interesting and useful.

Clinker Boatbuilding by John Leather
This book describes clinker and cold-moulded construction methods for sailing, rowing and power boats up to 20 feet in length. Every stage in the process is covered, from preparation, tools, materials, plans, keel structure, planking, frames, centreboards and decks to finishing off the hull, masts and oars. There are also specifications for three different clinker boats which can be built at home by the amateur.
Published by Adlard Coles Nautical. ISBN: 978-0-7136-3643-7

Boatbuilding Techniques Illustrated by Richard Birmingham
Covers a range of techniques and skills needed when constructing a boat, from interpreting the plans to hints on working different timbers. The author answers many of those puzzling questions, which need to be solved, in a clear manner. This book is a useful reference to the home builder or a newly trained apprentice in a fitting out yard.
Published by Adlard Coles Nautical. ISBN: 978-0-7136-7621-1

Illustrated Custom Boatbuilding by Bruce Roberts-Goodson
Catering specifically for the burgeoning one-off boatbuilding market, this book outlines the pros and cons of all practical boatbuilding materials, and gives advice on building the interiors, fitting engines and electrical systems for both sail and powerboats.
Published by Adlard Coles Nautical. ISBN: 978-0-7136-7749-2

Fitting Out Your Boat by Michael Naujok
This book is of interest to anyone fitting out a wooden or fibreglass hull from scratch, or for anyone wanting to renovate an old yacht and give it a facelift. It takes the DIY boat owner through the steps required, with the help of detailed photograph sequences and step-by-step instructions.
Published by Adlard Coles Nautical. ISBN: 978-0-7136-6806-3

Complete Amateur Boat Building by Michael Verney
A comprehensive book covering different types of boat construction.
Published by Adlard Coles Nautical. ISBN: 978-0-7136-5731-9

Practical Yacht Construction first published by Adlard Coles Nautical in 1947 and written by C J Watts who was for many years the chief draughtsman at Camper and Nicholsons' Southampton yard, has a wealth of information on traditional wooden yacht construction, and is well illustrated. There have been a number of reprints over the years.

The Sea-Boat, How to Build Rig and Sail her by Robert C Leslie and published by Chapman and Hall in 1892. This book explains how to construct a 16-foot open clinker-built boat.

In the UK, the monthly magazine *Classic Boat* frequently includes articles on tradition boats and their building while in the USA *Wooden Boat* magazine, published six times a year, has similar content and can be found on some UK bookstalls. The French magazine *Chasse Marée* also features traditional craft.

THE REGULATIONS

Since 16th June 1998, professionally constructed yachts from 2.5m to 24m may only be placed on the EEA (European Economic Area) market or used within the EEA if they conform to the Recreational Craft Directive (RCD). For the purposes of the regulations, boats are divided into four categories depending on their intended use. They are as follows:

Category A – Ocean: Designed for extended voyages where conditions may exceed wind force 8 (Beaufort scale) and significant wave heights of 4m and above but excluding abnormal conditions, and vessels largely self-sufficient.
Category B – Offshore: Designed for offshore voyages where conditions up to and including wind force 8 and significant wave heights up to and including 4m, may be experienced.
Category C – Inshore: Designed for voyages in coastal waters, large bays, estuaries, lakes and rivers where conditions up to and including wind force 6 and significant wave heights up to and including 2m, may be experienced.
Category D – Sheltered: Designed for voyages on sheltered coastal waters, small bays, small lakes, rivers and canals where conditions up to, and including, wind force 4 and significant wave heights up to and including 0.3m, may be experienced, with occasional waves of 0.5m maximum height, for example from passing vessels.

The regulations require boats to meet certain standards involving, among other things, such factors as stability, construction, maximum load, crew limit, maximum rated engine power and exhaust emissions. As far as the small boats considered in this book are concerned, only Categories C and D are relevant.

In the UK, many harbour, river and inland waterway authorities have regulations concerning navigation but in other coastal and offshore waters there are no restrictions on navigation. In certain other European countries, however, there are domestic laws which limit the area of operation of recreational craft depending on their RCD category. In France, for instance, boats in the RCD Categories C and D are restricted to limits within a certain distance of 'a safe haven'. So boats of these categories may, under UK regulations, sail where they like from the shores of the UK but if they enter French waters they may contravene domestic regulations having come from a point beyond that of 'a safe haven'. You can, however, trail your boat by road from the UK to France and sail her in French waters but not further from 'a safe haven' than the French regulations prescribe.

Information concerning the requirements of the RCD are available from a number of sources including the following:

The Department of Trade and Industry publishes a booklet entitled *Recreational Craft Guidance Notes on the UK Regulations (S.I. 2004/1464, as amended by S.I. 2004/3201)*, which explains the requirements of the Regulations in general terms but does not attempt to address detailed issues. It is available on the internet as a PDF file from http://www.bis.gov.uk/files/file11294.pdf.

The Regulations themselves can be obtained from:

The Office of Public Sector Information

London Office, Admiralty Arch, The Mall, London SW1A 2WH

They are also available free online at:

http://www.opsi.gov.uk/legislation/aboutlegislation.htm

Other sources of information and advice may be obtained from:

Royal Yachting Association

RYA House, Ensign Way, Hamble, Hants, SO31 4YA

Tel: 0845 365 0402/023 8060 4201; Fax: 023 8060 4289

PDF files are available from:

http://www.rya.org.uk/infoadvice/regssafety/Pages/recreationalcraftdirective.aspx

British Marine Industries Federation

Marine House, Thorpe Lea Road, Egham, Surrey TW20 8BF

Tel: 01784 473377; Fax: 01784 439678

E-mail: technical@britishmarine.co.uk

EXCEPTIONS

The Recreational Craft Directive regulations do not apply to amateur-built boats. However these may not be sold on the open market within the EEA within five years of completion without meeting RCD requirements. It is the responsibility of the builder to provide the documentation and information required to obtain the necessary category approval so it could be prudent for amateur builders to ensure their boats comply with the regulations and that they record details of the construction method and materials used.

The regulations do not apply to old boats or their replicas which means that traditional boats, designed before 1950, and individual replicas constructed using the same methods and materials as the original model may be built provided rules regarding certain safety and building standards are observed.

GLOSSARY

A

Abutt, butt up to
Place two pieces of frame side by side, edgewise. With the planks carefully positioned alongside each other, regular seams can be formed, which will mean they won't leak.

Accommodation space
Interior layout of the various spaces on a boat: cabins, saloon, lockers, etc.

Adze
Sharp tool with a curved handle, whose curved blade enables timbers to be trimmed and smoothed. The adze is an axe with a transverse blade.

Aligned ribs
This describes ribs or frames situated at the ends of the boat that don't follow a perpendicular plane to the keel, but rather a perpendicular plane to the planks.

Apron
Interior reinforcement timber, positioned either side of the stem, like a cheek piece on large vessels, to which the planking is nailed.

Auger
Piercing (hole making) tool comprised of a spiral bit and a perpendicular handle enabling you to turn it using both hands.

B

Beam

Transverse beam between the two sides of a vessel, supporting the deck. Usually referred to as a deck beam. Beam is generally used to designate the width of the boat at her widest station.

Bilge stringer
Longitudinal strake, passing across the ends of the floors.

Bitts
Pair of large vertical timbers from keel up through foredeck, used to secure anchor cable.

Blious
A vernacular term used in lower Brittany to designate a pasty mixture prepared using linseed oil, mastic, red lead paint, whiting and chopped oakum.

Board
Timber directly obtained by sawing a trunk lengthwise. The widest and longest boards are sought after for use as planks.

Boat shop, boatyard, yard
The construction workshop.

Body plan
Plan of the hull viewed on one side from the stern and the other from the bows, showing waterlines, sections at stations and diagonals.

Bolt rope
Reinforcing rope sewn into the edge of the sail to absorb the stress exerted on the canvas.

Boom
Spar along the foot of the mainsail.

Brace
Diagonal reinforcement piece fixed onto two elements of the frame to maintain their angular shape.

Breasthook
Curved timber used to reinforce and link the stem and the hull, level with the gunwale.

Bucking iron
Metal tool designed to turn things over in operations such as pegging and riveting.

Burr
A saucer-shaped copper washer fitted over the end of a copper boat nail before it is burred over (riveted or clenched). Also known as a rove or roove.

Burr set
A riveting tool used to drive on the rove or burr.

Butt block (or strap)
Piece of wood or metal positioned inside the hull, between two frames, covering two plank butt ends.

Butt end/End part
End of a piece of frame or planking; also called the end piece.

C

Camber
Transverse curve of a deck beam (or the deck itself), whose centre is higher than the ends.

Canvas
Cover laid decks and/or coachroof with canvas before painting to make watertight.

Carlins
Fore and aft timbers between deck beams and supporting edges of hatchways.

Caulk, to
Fill the seams between the planking with caulking cotton or oakum with the help of a caulking iron.

Caulking iron
A tool enabling the caulker to introduce a cord of oakum into the seams so as to make them watertight.

Ceilings
Set of interior planks forming a cladding for the hull. It protects the cargo or the accommodation space from dampness.

Centreboard
A pivoted wooden or sheet metal plate, which swings down through the keel to help limit the boat's leeway. This deeper draught keeps you on course.

Centreboard or daggerboard case
Watertight case, reaching above the waterline, surmounting a slot made in the keel to enable the fin of a centreboard or daggerboard to pass through it.

Chine
The angle where hull side meets hull bottom. A boat built using flat sheets of plywood may have a single chine producing a 'hard chine' hull or multiple chines producing a multi-chine (usually double chine) hull. A round bilged hull has no chine, but may have a hard or soft turn to the bilge.

Clamp/stringer/strake
Interior strake pegged through the plank and ribs, designed to support the inwales.

Clench, to
To turn over the end of a boat nail, across the grain, so that it is sent back into the wood, hence clencher built as alternative term for clinker built. Clench nails are used in the laps of planks, but nails and roves are used in frames.

Clinker
Type of planking attached in such a way that each plank overlaps the previous one, like slates on a roof. Clinker planking, of Nordic origin, is used in preference to carvel planking, for craft seeking lightness and flexibility. Also known as lapstrake construction.

Coach screw
Large square or octagonal headed screw.

Coal tar
Coal tar with which boats are coated, is highly effective in protecting the hull against barnacles and algae, especially when used on fishing boats. Coal tar is applied under heat with a circular pure bristle paintbrush. Pitch is a more refined derivative of it.

Coaming
Upstand around openings (hatches, cockpit and superstructure), which prevents water from washing in.

Cockpit
The sunken area aft from which the helmsman steers and the crew work the sheets.

Counter
In contrast to a transom stern, the counter stern extends the hull past the rudder post in a long overhang.

Crack
A small longitudinal crack at the surface of the wood caused by drying out. Small cracks weaken the plank and it is hard to make watertight.

Cradle
Originally, this was a construction designed to support a vessel for her launch. Today it more widely designates a support built to the boat's size, which is used to support her as well as lift her onto the hard, beach her and transport her.

Crook
A piece of wood that has grown in a curve rather than being bent to shape. Stronger than a bent piece, crooks are used for frames, knees, breasthook and so on.

D

Dagger board
Wooden board or metal plate that lowers vertically through the keel to help limit the boat's leeway.

Deadwood
A generally solid piece of timber between the sternpost and the keel (aft deadwood), or the stem and the keel (forward deadwood).

Deck beam
Transverse timber supporting the deck and also serving to stiffen the whole structure by keeping the sides of the vessel apart.

Diagonals
On the plans of a boat's sections, lines at 45 degrees to the keel. These lines enable you to better appreciate the hull form when she's heeled over.

Dip the lug
Move the yard of a lugsail to leeward of the mast during a tack to achieve a better set on the new tack. If you are unable to dip the lug, the yard remains to windward of the mast and the sail doesn't set quite so well.

Dog
Heavy staple with pointed ends used to join two wooden timbers.

Dovetail joint
A name given to a fan shaped interlocking technique for two timbers; its form resembles a dove's fanned out tail.

Drawknife
Tool comprising a sharp blade and two handles used to draw the blade towards you to trim and shape timber. Contrary to that of the plane, the depth of the cut of the blade isn't adjustable.

E

Elbow
Curved piece of the frame situated at the turn of the bilge, ensuring the link between the bilge and top futtock. Also known as the knee.

End part/Butt end
End of a piece of frame or planking. Also known as the end piece

F

Fashion piece
Shaped pieces of wood thickening the transom to provide extra area for fastening plank ends.

Fastenings
The whole set of joining elements - pegs, tree nails/trunnels, galvanised spikes, nails, bolts - used to join the various parts of the frame.

Flare
Athwartships lateral outward curve of a timber. The flare can be intentional or due to a deformity. Also, the designed outward curve of the bow sections.

Flat-sawn
Cut into boards parallel to the axis (length) of the trunk and tangential in relation to the annular rings. It is today's most popular cutting method, whose failing is that it results in boards whose width is not constant and a large amount of the wood has fibres that are tangential to the cut. The cutting into quarters, which was practised many years ago, resulted in fibres being perpendicular to the cut. It resulted in narrower boards with more wastage, but greater stability of shape.

Floor
Lower timber of a frame, which joins together the two ribs across the keel, to which it is joined.

Footwell
Lower part of the cockpit.

Forefoot
Large piece of curved wood, extending forward from the keel, which joins it to the stem. Also designates the part of the hull situated along the keel-stem junction, even when the forefoot timber doesn't exist.

Frame centres
Indication of distance between the frames, for example "framed in oak on 6in centres..."

Frame, rib
Transverse hull timbers - generally frames are sawn and ribs steamed - comprising either a single piece of wood or several parts (the bottom futtocks, knees, top futtocks and ears).

Freeboard
The height of the hull above the water.

Free, to
To extract, free up a timber, a plank, from the position it formerly occupied. It also means to dig out the area around a knot or a flaw in the wood, to remove it and replace it with a wooden plug to fill the hole.

Frost split
Cleft created in trees by the frost, in the direction of the grain.

Futtock
On sawn, jointed frames, a piece of wood that extends out from the floor in the bilges: bottom futtock, or an extension of the knee: the top futtock.

G

Gaff
Spar supporting the head of a gaff sail.

Gaff jaws
Wooden forked end of gaff that pivots on the mast.

Galvanised spikes
Large forged nails with a diamond shaped head and a square body, used to plank vessels of carvel construction.

Garboard strake
The hull plank closest to the keel, which is fitted into the rabbet, a groove cut for this purpose. As the boat ages, this strake can move in the rabbet and may leak. The garboard is the most difficult plank to change.

Gauge
Small template enabling a constant measurement to be produced.

Graving piece
Small piece of new wood replacing a damaged section after the damaged piece has been removed.

Gudgeon
A metal ring in which a pintle sits to form a hinge for the rudder against the transom.

Gunter
Gaff sail whose very high peaked gaff extends the luff so as to form an almost triangular sail.

Gunwale
Strake that covers the heads of the ribs and joins them to the topmost plank.

H

Half beam
Short beam positioned between the inwale and the hatch carlins to support the deck.

Half model
Model sculpted from a block of wood (sometimes a stack of boards) showing one half (lengthwise) of the hull, enabling the boat builder to determine the shape of the boat on a reduced scale. Boards can be disassembled to show the shapes of the waterlines.

Halving joint
Assembly made by the overlaying of two timbers, each of which has had half its thickness cut away.

Head of sail
Side by which a gaff sail is laced to its gaff or a lugsail to its yard and the upper corner of a Bermudan sail, by which it is hoisted.

Heart
The central part of a section of timber.

Heel
Aft extremity of the keel on which the stern post sits. Also bottom of the mast where it sits in the mast step.

Hog
Fore and aft timber capping the keel.

Hollow
Hollow section in the surface of the wood, often due to the position of the board in the timber it's cut from.

Hollow out
Hollow out the interior of a plank with the help of a plane with a rounded sole and blade, to perfectly adapt to the frame onto which it is nailed. The bilge stringers must be hollowed out.

Hounds (cheeks)
The point on the mast where the upper endsof the shrouds are attached.

I

Inwale
Interior stringer made of wood, which joins together the frames or ribs at deck level and receives the ends of the beams, which are jointed into it (beam shelf). The inwale/frame/sheer plank assembly is hard to bend out of shape and contributes a great deal to the boat's solidity. The inwale can be doubled up with a counter-beam or a sub-beam.

J

Jackplane
Long plane with a handle, which can be operated with both hands to smooth long timbers.

K

Keel
Main piece of the backbone serving as a base for the construction of a boat; the stem is fixed to its forward extremity and the stern post to its aft extremity.

Keelson
Longitudinal timber positioned inside the boat on top of the floors, reinforcing the keel onto which it is pegged.

Kevel
Upper extension of the frames, above the deck. The bulwark is fixed onto the kevels and in some cases they are used for belaying warps.

King plank
Centreline plank of a laid deck, set into the deck beams and designed to receive the joggled ends of the deck planks.

Knee
Curved supporting or binding timber cut from wood with a curved grain, often at the junction between a branch and the trunk of a tree, designed to bring together or strengthen the angle formed by joining two timbers.

Knight heads
Extensions that double up the stem, fixed directly against it, on both sides, extending from the rabbet, providing a greater surface area for attaching the plank ends and supporting the bowsprit. Another meaning is an external longitudinal reinforcement timber of the anchor fairlead/davit.

L

Lanolin
Grease from sheep's wool used as waterproof lubricant.

Lap clamps
Large wooden clips used as a joint clamp to hold together two overlapped clinker planks during the riveting operation.

Length Between Perpendiculars (LBP)
The length between a perpendicular dropped from the fore side of the stemhead and one from the after side of the rudder post. This length would be considerably less than the boat's overall length if she has a counter stern.

Limber hole
Notch or hole made in or through the lower section of a floor to enable the water in the boat's bilges to drain away to the bilge sump or the bilge, from where it will be pumped out.

Lodging knee
Horizontal knee placed each side of a deck beam against the frame to distribute the compression stress on the hull.

Loft, to
To lay out and draw at full scale.

Log
Uncut timber, covered with its bark.

M

Mast band
Metal band around mast to carry upper ends of shrouds and other rigging.

Mast step
Point where the mast attaches to the keelson with a mortise joint. On a small boat, the step consists of a single piece of mortised wood.

Middle futtock
Curved frame timber, situated at the turn of the bilge, to reinforce join between the bottom and top futtocks.

Midship section
Hull section at the point of maximum beam.

Mortise
Female element in the form of a slot from a mortise and tenon joint.

Mortise chisel
A kind of chisel for making grooves or mortises.

N

Nail punch
Tool used for driving the head of the nail deeper into a timber.

O

Oakum
Hemp tow used to caulk seams before paying them to make them watertight. Made from the remains of hemp after having the fibres stripped from it for making ropes.

P

Panel
Piece of canvas whose width depends on the weave; to make a sail you join the panels together.

Partners
A reinforcing pair of timbers placed either side of the mast at deck level or (in dinghies) a hole made in the deck or thwart for the mast to pass through. On unstayed lugsail craft, the partners alone ensure the mast is held upright.

Peak
Top corner of a gaff sail furthest from the mast.

Peak up
Lift up the peak of a gaff sail or the yard of a lugsail to help the sail set smoothly.

Pig
Block of cast iron or lead used as ballast.

Pintle
A pin that slips into a gudgeon (cf) to form a hinge on which the rudder turns against the transom.

Pitch, tar
A mixture of resin and coal tar poured under heat over the oakum, by means of a special spoon with a pouring lip, to make deck seams watertight.

Plan
Representation of a boat's shape, sail area and accommodation, via a reduced scale drawing.

Plan view
Hull form drawn and viewed from above.

Plank
A length of timber used to cover the framework of the hull in carvel or clinker construction. As a verb, to plank a hull is to cover the framework with clinker of carvel planking.

Planking
Originally referred to each of the planks covering the frame of the hull. Several planks laid end to end, from forward to aft, forming a strake. Today, we often use the word 'planking' to designate the exterior hull covering as a whole and the word 'plank' to designate each board. Carvel planking and clinker planking are the two most widely used techniques.

Profile plan
Drawing showing shape of boat from the side.

Prop/shore
Prop up a boat with angled timbers: the shores or props.

Q

Quarter sawn
Old method of cutting wood, resulting in wood fibres lying perpendicular to the cut. Its complexity is the reason it has been shelved to the benefit of the flat-sawn method.

R

Rabbet
Groove made in the entire length of the keel, on each side, to accommodate the garboard, as well as on the stem and stern post to receive the butt ends of the planking.

Rib, frame
Transverse hull timbers - generally frames are sawn and ribs steamed - comprising either a single piece of wood or several parts (the bottom futtocks, knees, top futtocks and ears).

Ribbon construction
Construction method consisting of positioning stringers - long wooden battens - onto a small number of templates (sometimes solely on that of the midship section) and fixed onto the longitudinal centreline structure, to define the form of the boat and the intermediate frames. It's also an operation that consists of offering up a stringer to check the perfect setting up of the frame, so that no frames are too short or too long.

Rig, rigging
Assembly of masts, yards, sails, ropes and blocks on a boat. The running rigging also comprises the sheets used to set and orientate the sails and spars: halyards, sheets, guys, topping lift, etc. The standing rigging is fixed and is used to hold up the masts and spars.

Rivet

Metal (usually copper) nail put through two pieces of wood and secured by fitting a washer (called a rove) and then hammering the end of the nail over. Riveting is a joining technique particularly used in clinker construction and in the case of steamed frames.

Rocker

Fore and aft upward curve of a dinghy's keel.

Rot

This is the blight of wood. You can easily differentiate between dry rot, which reaches the wood in the structure itself through the development of fungus whose branched strands – mycelium – break up the wood, and wet rot which affects wood that is poorly ventilated. Fresh water, rain water or condensation lead to the creation of localised rot.

Rove or roove

A saucer-shaped copper washer fitted over the end of a copper boat nail before it is burred over (riveted). Also known as a burr.

Rubbing strake

Protective stringer in the form of a strip placed on the outside of the hull, generally level with the sheer plank.

Rudder

Moveable board that serves to steer the vessel.

Rudder stock

Vertical section of the rudder, made of wood or metal, into which the iron fittings – pintles and gudgeons – are fitted, in the case of a transom hung rudder, or passing up through the counter in the rudder trunk. It's the rudder stock to which the action of the tiller is applied.

Rudder trunk

Metal tube passing through the counter to make a watertight fit for the rudder stock.

S

Samson post

Large vertical timber from keel up through foredeck, used to secure anchor cable.

Sapwood

Soft whitish part of the wood, located between the hard wood (or heartwood) and the bark, which is easy for insects and fungus to attack and which must be removed for boat construction.

Scale

Relationship between the boat's actual size and its representation on the plan, given in terms of a percentage, centimetres per metre (cpm) or as a ratio.

Scantlings

The dimensions of individual timbers used in a vessel's construction.

Scarf, Scarfing

Joining of two or several timbers to make one whole piece. Two ends to be joined are tapered and overlapped, then glued together.

Scupper

Opening in the bulwark, as far as the top of the gunwale, to enable the water shipped onto the deck to drain away.

Seam

Gap between edges of the hull or deck planking, designed to be caulked to make watertight. More generally designates the line formed between two strakes.

Section
Plane representing a section of the boat: longitudinal, cross, horizontal (waterlines).

Setting up
Check the port and starboard symmetry of a frame: a plumbline positioned in the middle of the frame must fall exactly along the axis of the keel.

Shape
Hollow out the internal face of a plank to adapt it to the round part of the frame, at the bilge for example.

Sheave hole
Opening or rectangular port made through a mast or spar, into which a sheave is placed, in order to run a rope through it.

Sheer line
The sheer line corresponds with the fore and aft curve of the deck, generally raised at the forward and aft extremities.

Sheer strake
Topmost planking strake, which is larger than the others and gives line and shape to the boat's sheer. Linked with the inwale either side of the frames, the top strake gives the hull great stiffness.

Shore/prop
Prop up a boat by shoring her up with angled timbers: the shores or props.

Shutter plank
Last piece of planking to be positioned, generally at the turn of the bilge, to finish off the hull. Great care must go into its fitting.

Side deck
Section of the deck on either side of the hatch or cabin superstructure.

Sole
Bottom boards of a flat boat or the 'floor' of the cabin or cockpit.

Spar
General term for a mast, yard, gaff, boom, pole, sprit, etc.

Species of wood
The most frequently used in the marine environment are broad-leaved trees, regional hardwoods like the oak, elm, ash, acacia, chestnut; coniferous trees like pitch pine, red fir, Douglas fir, Scots pine, Maritime pine, locally sourced pine; larch; spruce; tropical hardwoods like mahogany, teak, sapele, iroko, niangon, black afara... Dinghies and traditional working boats are generally constructed from locally sourced wood; yachts also use tropical hardwoods. Coniferous woods are used as much for the planking as the masts and spars.

Spile, to
To transfer a shape (of a plank or floor etc) directly onto the piece of wood to be cut to make that shape.

Spiling batten
A spiling batten or rule serves as a reference line from which to measure curves during spiling.

Sprit
Diagonal spar that serves to tension a sail. On a spritsail rig, the sprit runs from the tack to the peak of the mainsail.

Square
Cut a timber to give it a square or rectangular section.

Standing rigging
The shrouds, forestay and backstay – rigging that's permanently fixed at both ends and holds. the mast up.

Starboard
The righthand side of the boat, when you're looking forward; the opposite of port.

Stealer
Designates the short plank, in the shape of a triangle, joined to another plank to make it wider, generally in the aft section at the outward turn of the bilge.

Steam
To place the planks in a steam box: wooden or metal box (or tube) in which steam circulates, so as to subject them to damp heat, which makes the planks flexible and enables them to be bent without breaking.

Steamed timber
Wood that has been steamed to give it the necessary flexibility for it to be bent into the desired shape; for example a frame or a plank.

Stem
Main timber situated at the forward end of the keel. The stem, made from one or several timbers, is joined to the keel via the stem deadwood, on the inside, and sometimes the forefoot, on the outside.

Stepped scarf joint
The bevelled ends of two timbers to be joined are each cut into a step so that when overlaid they marry up and are locked so that they can't slide apart. Reminiscent of a lightning symbol side on. Used to make up a keel that is too long to be made from a single timber.

Stern post
This is the key timber at the after end of the keel. It is attached directly to the keel. The stern post is erected on the aft extremity of the keel and carries the rudder. A counter may extend out from it or it may directly support the transom. On canoe sterns, the planking joins onto the stern post.

Stopwater
Peg driven into a drilled hole through the joint between two frame timbers to ensure a watertight joint. The stopwater pegs are essentially positioned at the bottom of the rabbet and are covered by the planking butt ends.

Strake
The whole length of a plank, from one end of the hull to the other, even if it is made up of several parts.

Stringer
General term designating a longitudinal timber running from one end of a boat to the other.

Superstructure
Constructions sited above deck level: coachroof, wheelhouse, deckhouse.

T

Table of offsets
Table providing all the necessary measurements for lofting without having to find them from the lines plan.

Tan
Coat or soak the sails, either hot or cold, according to the method used, in a substance designed to protect against mildew and ensure their long life. For this you use ochre, oak bark...

Tar
A resinous material extracted from trees like pines, firs, larches; in this case it's a vegetable tar, like Norwegian tar. Mineral tar is a derivative of coal. It is used to coat ropes and, when heated, to coat hulls.

Template
Full scale wooden pattern, serving as a model to fashion various parts.

Tenon
Extremity of a timber, bevelled out into an octagonal or square form, designed to enter a (female) mortise to create a strong joint.

Throat
The upper corner near the mast on a gaff mainsail.

Toe rail
Slim vertical board fixed onto small posts to heighten the hull or bulwark. The timber can be fixed or removable. On open dinghies it is designed to prevent shipping water; on decked boats it has the function of a toe rail or guard rail.

Tonnage, registered
The net registered tonnage is a measure of the boat's internal capacity, minus certain 'spaces' such as that for navigation, which may be used for levying dues.

Topmast
Tapered section at the upper end of the mast, above the hounds, which sometimes carries a topsail. Some topmasts are a separate spar from the mast.

Torture
Force a plank over onto itself in a twisting motion.

Transom
Flat stern of the boat, which is vertical or raked and is made up of a single timber board or an assembly of planks.

Treenail, Trenail or trunnel
Long peg or pin made from a very hard wood used to fix the planking or timbers of vessels. The peg is introduced into a hole made beforehand; it is held in position by means of wedges. Today the use of pegs is reserved for the restoration of old boats.

Tuck
The underwater part of the stern at which the sides, bottom and transom merge together.

Upperworks
Set of structures forming the boat above the waterline; decks, coach house etc.

Vessel depth
Depth of the vessel, which is measured at the maximum beam, from the top of the keelson or keel timber, to the deck.

Waterlines
Horizontal sections on a design plan, drawn parallel to the waterline, showing the hull shape at set distances above and below the actual designed waterline.

Wedging
To wedge a plank into place is to force it to bend along its edge, in the direction of its width.

Yard, boatyard, boat shop
The construction workshop.

INDEX

L

M

O

P

R

S

T

W

ACKNOWLEDGEMENTS

Drawings and plans: Jean-François Garry

Photos:

p 74: Andre Conan

pp 8, 100, 104: Bernard Ficatier

pp 47, 50, 53 (top), 53 (bottom), 54, 55, 57, 58, 60, 61, 65, 69, 70, 71, 73 (left), 85, 86, 91, 97, 107: Francis Holveck

pp 49, 51, 75 (top), 75 (bottom), 80: Michel Le Coz

pp 48, 76: Andre Linard

p 35: Catherine Nourry

pp 4, 68, 83: Philippe Roy/ Hoa-qui/ Eyedea Illustration

pp 45, 73 (right), 73 (middle right), 73 (bottom right), 77, 80 (left), 87 (top), 87 (bottom), 93 (top), 93 (bottom), 94 (top), 94 (bottom), 95 (top), 95 (bottom), 101, 106: Reserved rights

The following have contributed to this work: *Chasse-Marée*, Jean-Pierre Abraham, Claude Hascoet, Edith Kerespars, Kim Savina. The authors would particularly like to thank Martine Garry for her collaboration.

Adlard Coles Nautical would like to thank Kathy Mansfield for the translation of this work from French to English and to Peter Cook for his checking of the English version prior to publication.